Part 1:
Scrum Fundamentals

*A Beginner's Guide to Mastery of The
Scrum Project Management Methodology*

Jeff Cohn

no scenarios in which the publisher or the original author of this work can be in any fashion deemed liable for any hardship or damages that may befall them after undertaking information described herein.

Additionally, the information in the following pages is intended only for informational purposes and should thus be thought of as universal. As befitting its nature, it is presented without assurance regarding its prolonged validity or interim quality. Trademarks that are mentioned are done without written consent and can in no way be considered an endorsement from the trademark holder.

Part 1: Table of contents

Introduction

Thank you very much for purchasing, "*Scrum Fundamentals. A beginner's guide to mastery of the Scrum project management methodology.*" It's really exciting to see that you are interested in learning more about Agile methodologies, in particular, Scrum.

If you are new to project management, then you are about to discover a new world filled with many possibilities. Project management is not an easy area to master since many factors come into play when you are embarking upon a new journey such this one.

If you are a veteran of project management, but new to Scrum, then I think you will find an interesting way in which you can improve your current knowledge of project management methodologies and how this book can allow you to find new tools.

If you are familiar with Scrum, then I hope this book can serve you as a refresher, but also help you reflect on how you can build on your existing knowledge of Scrum and the various elements that go into this methodology.

When you begin learning about the Agile world, you begin to uncover the different possibilities that can become unlocked by a simple shift in mindset. Now, one of the most common misconceptions is that one project management methodology is better than another. And that is simply not true.

This isn't a question about which methodology is better. This is about understanding the applications that Agile, in particular, Scrum, have in certain projects as compared to others.

As such, when you think about Agile, think about how your projects may benefit from a methodology that contemplates change and uncertainty as a part of the normal course of the project.

Does that sound familiar?

You see, traditional project management methodologies contemplate a more stable working environment. These methodologies, such as the methodology espoused by the Project Management Institute, are ideal for those environments in which there are much more stable conditions. For instance, think about projects which have already been done many times before.

Therefore, traditional project management methodologies are great for those projects which have set rules and guidelines in place. For instance, road constructions, buildings, social programs are all examples of how traditional project management methodologies can be utilized to achieve the objectives of the stakeholders in the project.

Now, what about those projects which have

tight deadlines, uncertain conditions, and continuous change?

This is where Agile shines.

Of course, most folks think of software development when they think of Agile and Scrum. While this is true, Agile methodologies have grown to such a point where they can be applied to a wide array of fields. In particular, Scrum can be implemented in those fields which have a high degree of uncertainty or when there is a considerable amount of change involved.

Agile is all about making a continuous improvement on a product/service, and how they are being delivered. This is a key difference.

In traditional project management methodologies, the deliverables aren't seen until the end of the project. In the case of Agile, the presentation of deliverables is incremental. What that means is that project stakeholders won't have to wait until the end of the project to see if the deliverables actually work.

With Scrum, the focus is on delivering incremental results so that effectiveness can be measured before the final delivery of the product. This means that Scrum practitioners will have the opportunity to fix things on the fly and not have to wait until after the project has concluded in order to fix any bugs in the final deliverables.

At this point, you might be asking yourself:

what is the difference between Agile and Scrum?

And, that is a fair question.

Agile is a philosophy, an approach, to project management. Agile is based on continuous improvement and a consistent search for improved quality. This led to the development of the Agile Manifesto.

The Agile Manifesto is a document which encompasses the spirit of Agile: getting improved results in the least amount of time possible, with continuous improvement on the quality of outputs.

Since Agile was born out of the software industry, it considers *time* as one of the most valuable resources that team members can learn to cherish and value.

Speaking of valuable resources, Agile methodologies place a high degree of value on *people*.

Unlike other project management approaches in which material resources are more valuable than people, Agile and Scrum place a large amount of focus on people and the role they play within the teams they belong to.

With Agile, a flat, non-hierarchical structure is considered to be the best way in which teams can be productive. The leadership roles played by the Scrum Master and the Product Owner are not to give orders, or even determine what needs to be done.

The roles of these leaders are more of a servant leadership in which they are motivated to provide their team members with everything they need in order to become successful and achieve the objectives set forth at the outset of the project.

As you can see, Scrum places a great deal of value on collaboration and teamwork rather than on "directing" and "guiding." While leaders certainly bear their share of responsibility, responsibility is shared by all members of the team. Therefore, if anything goes wrong, it's the team's collective responsibility. But, if everything goes right, it's the team's collective victory.

This attitude makes Scrum an incredibly collaborative methodology in which all team members are working together to reach the same goal. It should be said that members of a Scrum team should all be on the same page and subscribe to the same beliefs.

As such, this book looks to dig deeper into the elements that make Scrum a great project management methodology in which you, and your organization, can improve their collaborative nature. So, we will be really drilling down on the most important aspects of Scrum, and how you can apply them into your organization right away.

So, buckle up because we are going to be heading for quite a ride. I am sure you will enjoy every bit of it.

Chapter 1: Introduction to Agile and Its Principles

In the first chapter of this book, we are going to be taking a closer look at what Agile is, and its underlying principles. Like any other philosophies, there are concepts, principles, axioms, and tents which guide the activities that are to be conducted under the umbrella of this methodology.

As such, we are going to be drilling down on the definition of Agile, its 12 principles and we are even going to talk a little bit about this history of Agile. So, let's get started.

Defining Agile

Our starting point for this discussion in the definition of Agile. In the introduction, we used the terms "Agile" and "Scrum" rather interchangeably, though they are two completely different concepts.

First of all, Agile is all about adapting to change. It is about being able to adapt and succeed in an uncertain and turbulent environment.

As we stated earlier, Agile methodologies are focused on thriving in situations in which projects don't always have a stable environment.

So, what does it mean to be in an uncertain and turbulent environment?

It means that there are lots of questions surrounding your tasks with little to no clarity on stability.

Now, before you panic and head for the door, allow me to elaborate.

In the introduction, I mentioned how there are projects which experts basically have down cold.

Think of construction.

When engineers build a road, they have a clear idea about what specifications are needed to the materials to be used, they are aware of the topography and have a very good idea about the costs associated with the project. Since road construction has been around for a while, there is a great deal of information on how to deal with the potential risks that come with this task.

So, traditional project management methodologies are ideal for this type of task since there are predictable outcomes, predictable inputs, and predictable processes. Sure, there is always the risk for some unforeseen or even fortuitous event which may derail a project, but that's a bit unlikely.

Now, let's consider a technical project, that could be any type of technology and not just software. The uncertainty is born out of the fact that you are producing something that's never been done before or applied in a certain way to the nuances of your project/organization.

Can you see where the uncertainty lies?

In this case, in projects that lead to outcomes which have never produced before, you can't truly anticipate everything that will happen. But you must be prepared to deal with changes as they happen. For instance, you believe that there is a good way of doing something, but as you test the technology, it doesn't run the way you thought it would. So, you need to find another way of making it work properly.

Based on this logic, Scrum is an ideal way for project managers to find a project management methodology which can espouse change without having to resort to complex procedures in order to get all the stakeholders involved to sign off on each move. This makes the process more "Agile" and thereby reduces the time and effort needed to make shifts as per conditions.

A Brief History of Scrum

Project management is hardly new.

As a matter of fact, traditional project management was born out of the experiences that project professionals had as a result of their work in various fields. Since project management was largely experienced-based, it wasn't always easy for project managers to deal with the myriad of aspects that go into completing a project successfully.

Over time, project management became more systematic in such a way that experiences were collected and built into a framework that could be used as a reference for future work done in similar fields.

This collection of knowledge, experience, and lessons learned led to the creation of the traditional project management approaches known today. In particular, the methodology espoused by the Project Management Institute.

While there is nothing wrong with this methodology, the software industry realized that traditional project management approaches just weren't cutting it for them. There had to be something more suited to the needs and characteristics of the software industry which could provide a more dynamic framework.

And so, the nineties brought about innovations in the field of programming and software development. One of the new methods that emerged is known as "extreme programming" or XP. This led to one of the most popular versions of the Windows operating system known as "Windows XP."

Extreme programming became one of the precursors to what would eventually become known as Agile. Considering that Agile was born out of the software industry, Agile project management methodologies became synonymous with the software industry.

In the late nineties, some of the most successful software developers and programmers began putting their heads together in order to come up with a brand-new approach which could encompass the needs and characteristics of the software industry.

This led to the emergence of the Agile Manifesto in 2001.

The Agile Manifesto

The group of 17 minds which came together to develop the Agile Manifesto was intent on building a list of ideas and concepts in a framework which could serve their own industry. Nevertheless, the Agile Manifesto wasn't just about the software industry; it was intended to have a cross-cutting appeal which could lead it to be applied to virtually any known industry.

The Agile Manifesto is a collection of 12 principles which encompass the Agile philosophy. They make up the core and the backbone of all Agile methodologies in such a way that they are the guiding tenets on which Agile methodologies are founded on.

Since 2001, the Agile movement has grown into a series of methodologies which can be applied to a given number of roles. In that regard, Scrum is the one which has the most cross-cutting appeal. This is the kind of methodology which can be implemented in virtually any field, particularly, those that have a high degree of uncertainty and even volatility.

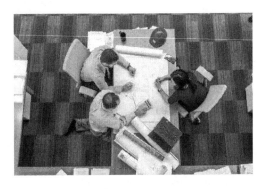

Therefore, Agile should be seen as a mindset more than a collection of steps which make up a procedure.

That's the case of traditional project management.

If you are looking for a collection of steps that must be implemented in succession without much consideration on how to innovate or implement change, then you should take a long look at how Scrum can also be used in a systematic and formulaic way.

Consequently, Agile has a little bit of everything for everyone. You won't have to guess at anything. However, Agile does require you to often think outside the box and not within a rigid structure. By freeing your mind, you will be able to see the forest for the trees and really find the best and most creative way of doing things.

This led the Agile Manifesto to become a declaration in which its creators stated the following:

"We are uncovering better ways of developing software by doing it and helping others do it. Through this work, we have come to value:

Individuals and interactions *over processes and tools*

Working software *over comprehensive documentation*

Customer collaboration *over contract negotiation*

Responding to change *over following a plan*

That is, while there is value in the items on the right, we value the items on the left more."

As you can see, the Agile Manifesto is a declaration in which its authors wanted to make clear what they value and where they stand on the development of outputs.

Of course, it should be noted that the Agile Manifesto explicitly talks about software and its development though we have clearly stated that from its software beginnings Agile is now applicable to virtually all fields.

Notice how Agile values people more than processes and tools. While processes and tools are important, Agile believes that people hold a greater value. The same can be said about working software, that is, a working output, over documentation that covers the project itself. Sure, there is paperwork to be dealt with, but rather than spending large amounts of time preparing complex reports and manuals that will probably have to been changed again in no time, focus on getting something valuable as a deliverable out to your customers.

The last two points in the Agile Manifesto refer to change and customer collaboration. This is important since engagement with the customer is essential in making sure that the outputs developed, meet the customer's expectations. Responding to change not only refers to what the customer wants but also what the circumstance may dictate. Therefore, Agile is all about flexibility and adaptability rather than setting everything in stone and "perfecting" the way things are done.

Now that Agile is a considered to be a full-fledged project management framework, it's worth looking at the principles which guide its implementation and development.

Principle #1: Our highest priority is to satisfy the customer through early and continuous delivery of valuable software.

This principle speaks for itself. The main idea behind this first principle is to meet the customer's expectation, but also to deliver working software early on in the development of the final product. This is an important difference over traditional project management methodologies as traditional approaches usually leave delivery of outputs until the end of the project. This often leads to issues along the way that could have been resolved early on but end up being addressed at the end.

This principle is applicable to all fields. It is quite possible to deliver results in advance of the release of the final output. By doing this, it enables the customer and project stakeholders to see where problems may lie, and how to address them before the final output is released.

As such, the starting point is to ensure customer satisfaction above all.

Principle #2: Welcome changing requirements, even late in development. Agile processes harness change for the customer's competitive advantage.

In traditional project management methodologies, change is discouraged as traditional project management tries to establish predictable processes as much as possible. The reason for this is rooted in the desire to eliminate uncertainty which can increase risk.

In the realm of Agile, change is welcome even if it is very late in the game. Of course, ground rules need to be set in order to govern change management. Nevertheless, Agile opens the door for changes to be made. After all, it's all about delivering the type of product which will give the customer an edge over their competition.

Consequently, Agile teams need to keep an open mind that leads them to figure out how to incorporate change without becoming clogged up with the reason why a change shouldn't be made. That is why providing deliverables at different stages are vital for successful project management.

Principle #3: Deliver working software frequently, from a couple of weeks to a couple of months, with a preference to the shorter timescale.

Once again, Agile is bent on providing outputs as early as possible. When this happens, the customer can see what is being done. Therefore, this improves the quality of the communication and feedback that development teams can get on their work.

Thus, Agile teams should be encouraged to produce deliverables as early as possible in order to ensure that potential issues can be addressed well ahead of time and dealt with accordingly.

Principle #4: Business people and developers must work together daily throughout the project.

This principle underscores the highly collaborative nature of Agile. Rather than leaving the customer out of the development process, Agile encourages the customer's input and feedback as much as possible throughout the development cycle of the project.

In addition, the roles of the leaders in an Agile environment is to maintain constant communication with development teams in order to ensure that they have all of the resources they need while addressing any limitations that may have arisen from the normal course of action.

Principle #5: Build projects around motivated individuals. Give them the environment and support they need and trust them to get the job done.

Earlier, when I made a point of Agile being a mindset, I had this principle in mind.

When you think about "motivated individuals" it isn't just about people who want to work and get things done. That's not enough.

In Agile, the mindset needs to be focused on getting the job done in the best possible way, especially if that entails coming up with a novel solution. After all, creativity is at the heart of innovation. But this only happens when individuals are truly engaged with the role; they play on the team they are on.

So, motivation is built on empowering individuals to take control of their own area of responsibility. Bear in mind that Agile places greater value on individuals rather than processes. So, fostering individuals is at the core of developing an Agile mindset.

Principle #6: The most efficient and effective method of conveying information to and within a development team is a face-to-face conversation.

It should be noted that technology has made communication so much easier especially when teams are not physically located together. Nevertheless, the best means of communication is still a face-to-face conversation.

This is a vital point since the co-location of teams allows for an improved collaborative environment. So, I hope that you are beginning to see a trend in the underlying philosophy that makes up an Agile team and environment.

Principle #7: Working software is the primary measure of progress.

This one is a biggie. After all, the only way you can truly measure the success of a project is through the achievement of the projects deliverable(s). If you are unable to deliver what you set out to deliver, then the project is essentially a failure.

Naturally, the Agile principles themselves make an explicit mention of working software though this can be applied to any type of field in which there is an output that is to be produced. When your team is able to produce such deliverables, then you can gauge if your projects have actually met the expectations it was set out to meet.

One important thing to note is, if for some reason, project deliverables are not met, and then any issues can be addressed in the subsequent phase of the project. Therefore, the development team will have the opportunity to deal with it in time. While that may entail some additional work, it will go a long way toward solving the overall issue.

Principle #8: Agile processes promote sustainable development. The sponsors, developers, and users should be able to maintain a constant pace indefinitely.

The point of "sustainable development" is all about being realistic. When project teams develop a given tempo, they are expected to maintain it over long periods of time, or indefinitely. This is an essential quality of Agile.

When teams develop a realistic tempo which they can maintain over long periods of time, they will be able to achieve a high level of performance. But it should also be noted that teams are discouraged from working "too fast" or "too hard" as this would lead to an unsustainable pace. Ultimately, an unsustainable pace would lead teams to burnout and potentially create more problems than solutions.

Principle #9: Continuous attention to technical excellence and good design enhances agility.

When teams are able to continuously perfect their systems, procedures and technical expertise, projects will become easier and easier while being completed in a shorter period of time. This is why Agile fosters an environment in which development teams should be collaborative and kept together as much as possible.

As long as development teams can remain together and develop their capabilities in tandem, they will be able to make faster progress. Ultimately, development teams will have their processes down to such a point where it becomes second-nature.

However, the adaptable nature of Agile does not afford development teams too much time to get comfortable.

Principle #10: Simplicity - the art of maximizing the amount of work not done - is essential.

By learning that work not done is just as important as the work that is actually done, teams can become highly efficient. They are able to get a clear sense of what can be done and the best way in which they can minimize the amount of work that goes into achieving a given task.

That being said, it's important for project leaders to understand the need to cut out unnecessary work. A simple example of this is documentation. Agile espouses an approach in which voluminous documentation is discouraged in favor of the simple reporting which can provide project stakeholders with the right idea about where the project is headed.

Principle #11: The best architectures, requirements, and designs emerge from self-organizing teams.

On the subject of self-organizing teams, Agile is all about letting development teams work things out amongst themselves. In contrast to traditional project management in which leaders dictate the work to be done, Agile is focused on letting teams figure out what they need to do and the best way to do it. This allows for creativity to breed the best possible solutions to the problems at hand.

Principle #12: At regular intervals, the team reflects on how to become more effective, then tunes and adjusts its behavior accordingly.

The last principle of the Agile philosophy considers the need to reflect and improve upon mistakes. As with anything in life, nothing is perfect. That is why development teams working under the Agile flag need to consider the importance of sitting down and going over the good and bad in each development phase. This fosters an environment of accountability among all stakeholders in such a way that there is no need to have one leader bearing down on everyone else.

The feedback loop that is created within an Agile environment allows for teams to become closer and develop the type of collaboration which is essential in getting the job done in the best possible manner.

Well, that was quite a bit of information we dealt with in this chapter. I would encourage you to go over the principles presented herein as Agile begins with a fundamental shift in your and your organization's mindset. Even if you don't deal with projects in the traditional sense of the word, you can still implement an Agile mindset in such a way that your organization will become more open to change.

The most important thing to keep in mind is that your team is the most valuable resource you have at your disposal. Therefore, giving teams the freedom to self-organize is one of the most important success factors when working within an Agile approach.

Chapter 2: Breaking Down A Scrum Project

In this chapter, we will be looking at how a Scrum project actually works and the way that Scrum can be put to the test. So, we are going to be taking a look at how a Scrum project begins, where it is born, and an overview of the different parts and stages of the project.

In addition, we will be looking at the main components of a Scrum project. That way, you can become aware of the different inputs that a successful Scrum project needs in order to achieve its goals.

So, then let's get started.

What is a Project?

In short, a project is a temporary action that will produce a permanent outcome.

Based on that logic, a project is a response to a problem, or need, which has motivated those affected to seek a permanent solution through a temporary action.

Let's consider a classic situation.

Two towns are divided by a river. In order for folks to go from one town to the next, they need to drive for about an hour in order to go around the river. However, the closest route between both towns, which is crossing the river, would take 10 minutes.

So, both towns have agreed to build a bridge to connect both towns so that folks from both towns can easily reach both sides. In addition, each town has agreed to pay for half of the cost of building the bridge.

A commission was created with members from both towns to come up with a project to get the bridge completed. After meetings, the commission has decided what they want, where they want it and a rough estimate of how long it would take to get it done.

The commission also met with contractors who pitched their ideas and plans. After careful consideration, one contractor was selected. This contractor got to work and built the bridge in three months. The contract was paid for their construction work but agreed to sign a contract for the maintenance of the bridge.

In the end, the project was a success; flow between both towns increased, investment picked up, and everyone came out a winner.

In this example, we see a problem, which is a river dividing both towns thereby forcing them to drive a long way around to reach the other side. As a result, business wasn't as good as it could be, and folks were discouraged from visiting the other town.

The solution was to build a bridge. The temporary action was the construction of the building itself. After all, construction was completed in three months. We don't expect the construction of the building to be ongoing forever. We expect the construction to be over in a given period of time and the final product to be delivered.

As such, the temporary action (the construction of the bridge), provided a permanent solution to the problem (the bridge itself). This is a clear example of how a project is nothing more than a temporary action.

Yet, there is a great deal of work that goes into building the bridge itself. There is labor, and there are resources, (time, money, materials) which are needed in order to make the project a reality. Therefore, it's up to the project managers to do their best in order to make the project bear the fruit that it was intended to.

In this example, we chose a rather predictable output, as a bridge construction is hardly a new endeavor. Of course, engineers and planners have taken it upon themselves to make new designs and attempt different approaches. Some have worked while others have not. Nevertheless, the important thing is that out of a seemingly perfected process there is still the initiative for growth and change.

In those fields in which there is much less certainty (software development, pharma, biotech, social programs) there is far less predictability. Consequently, project managers need to find the best way in which they can deliver results as early as possible and make sure that these results are sustainable throughout the life of the project. This is where Agile really shines.

Project Phases

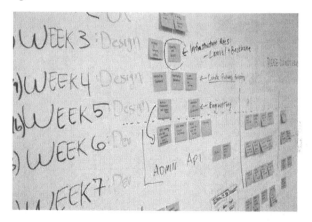

Projects are typically conceived as a process that must be followed in order to achieve a final output successfully. This is an important consideration as project managers tend to make an effort to systematize processes in order to remove as much risk and uncertainty as possible.

While it is true that risk is an inherent part of any project, working with clear guidelines and within a proper framework can reduce a great deal of risk. However, projects tend to have dynamic natures in which anything can happen.

As such, projects generally have five phases. Let's get into detail regarding each one.

1.   **Planning**. The first phase of any project is the planning phase. In this phase, project managers will sit down the project sponsors and stakeholders in order to determine what the objectives are intended for the project. This is the part where interested parties will sit down, hammer out contracts, and come to agreements on what is going to be delivered, under what timeline and what the acceptance criteria for the project will be. This phase also considers the formation of project teams.

2.   **Initiation**. The second phase of a project involves the necessary prep work that will go into putting the project into motion. This could include the purchase of equipment, hiring of staff, and the acquisition of any other materials which will be needed in order to make the project happen. Also, negotiations may be conducted with suppliers as needed.

3.   **Execution**. This phase is all about getting the job done. So, the project teams will come together to actually work and get the project moving. Depending on the project management methodology, you might get some early results such as in the of Agile, or deliverables will be seen until

the end of the project such as in the case of more traditional project management approaches. This is the phrase in which the objectives begin to come to fruition.

4.   **Monitoring and evaluation.** When the project reaches this phase, it is because the final output has been released and is undergoing testing. It is at the point that the final deliverables are tested to make sure they meet the required specifications before the final acceptance of the products. This phase may lead to the customer rejecting the final product and requesting changes before the final product is accepted.

5.   **Closing.** Once the products have been accepted, then the project will go into the closing phase. When the project enters this phase, any final changes are made to the deliverables, and the customer gives the final acceptance to the products. This is where the ribbon is cut, and all the applauses come. The final release of the product is issued, and there are high fives all around. The project team then begins to wind everything up and either move on to the next project or say goodbye.

This process described above is the typical lifecycle of the project. This type of process can normally be seen with traditional project management methodologies. In such cases, you will notice that testing and acceptance happens at the end of the entire project cycle. This means that the customer will not have any indication of what the final product will look like until the end of the project itself.

This approach opens the door for a series of issues since the project team will not be clear on what will happen when the customer sees the final output. As such, there is a very real possibility that the customer will not accept the final deliverables and ask for changes. When this happens, it can become catastrophic to the project team as having changes made to the deliverables once they have been assembled may lead to considerable cost and time overruns. Consequently, making sure that the final outputs are produced to the specifications of the client is essential in order to avoid any delays or even surprises at the end of the project.

How Does Scrum Play into All of This?

Scrum works in the exact same way as normal project work. The main difference between a traditional project and Scrum is in the mindset and attitude toward change, adaptability, and harnessing the power of change.

Naturally, Scrum begins with a planning phase that leads to the initiation phase. Once the project is off and running, the development team can come in and get to work. However, the main difference with Scrum is that the execution phrase is broken down into sections called "sprints." These sprints are designed to be phases in which the development team produce a certain aspect of the final output. At the end of the sprint, the customer should be able to see that part in action, in order to get a glimpse of what the final product will look like.

The monitoring and evaluation phase are integrated into each sprint in such a way that the development team can test the product and determine if there are mods which need to be made to ensure that everything is running fine. Finally, the closing phrase will lead to the customer accepting the final output and thereby bringing the project to an end.

Since every project is different, the project team needs to be prepared for anything that may come their way. This means keeping an open mind and ensuring that they have everything they need in order to become as successful as they possibly can. Nevertheless, care needs to be taken in ensuring that the most important aspects of the final output are respected.

As you can see, the biggest difference in terms of the organization that a Scrum project has compared to a traditional one, is that Scrum is focused on the customer, delivering value as early as possible and working out any potential bugs from the get-go. This ensures that all stakeholders will be aware of how the project is developing.

By addressing potential issues as early as possible, the project team can see if there might be any time or cost overruns and see how they may be addressed. Furthermore, the project team can determine what needs to be in order to avoid cost and time overruns. That way, the project can become successful, meet the acceptance criteria, and deliver on the overall objectives as stated.

Scrum Project Components

At this point, we are going to get into the specifics of the components which make up a Scrum project.

First of all, let's look at the players that make up a Scrum team.

• **Product Owner**. The Product Owner in a Scrum team is called "the voice of the customer." What this means is that the developers won't actually have any direct communication with the customer. That's the Product Owner's job. The Product Owner is the main person in charge of interacting with the customer in such a way that the Product Owner is able to relay the customer's vision and feedback to the rest of the team. This implies that the Product Owner is at the front line of the development process. And while the Product Owner has a key leadership role, they are not the boss.

• **Scrum Master**. The name of this player does not refer to "master" in terms of domain or leadership, but rather, it refers to the level of mastery in the Scrum methodology. As such, the

Scrum Master is the link between the Product Owner (the customer) and the Development Team. The role of the Scrum Master is that of subservient leadership. That is, the Scrum Master is very much engaged in providing guidance and leadership when needed but does not act like a "boss." Rather, the Scrum Master's role is to provide all of the necessary tools and elements which the Development Team needs in order to carry out their objectives.

- **Development Team**: The Development Team is the one in charge of actually putting the project into motion. These are the folks who actually carry out the work. In general, a Development Team consists of about 4 to 6 members. They generally work in a co-located setting, that is, in the same physical location under the guidance of the Scrum Master and Product Owner. The Development Team is also in charge of conducting product demos and technical explanations to the customer especially when the Product Owner is not the most qualified to deliver such information.

As you can see, the number of players in a Scrum team is rather small. As such, one of the biggest criticisms of Scrum is that it is not scalable particularly for very large and extensive projects. But that assertion could not be further from the truth.

When dealing with very large-scale projects, Scrum can be scaled in such a way that multiple Development Team teams work in tandem with multiple Scrum Masters in order to break up the work into a manageable chunk.

In fact, very large projects may have broader roles such as a Project Product Owner and a Project Scrum Master. These two roles would be in charge of making sure the entire project machinery works in tandem.

While we will get into further details about Scrum roles in later chapters, it's worth pointing out that the description we have provided herein helps to gain a better perspective of how Agile, and in particular Scrum, see the interaction between the various players throughout the lifecycle of the project.

It should also be noted that Scrum strives to achieve efficiency by having the greatest amount of work done with the least amount of staff.

Now, does this mean that staff will be pushed to the max?

Actually, no.

Bear in mind that Scrum advocates for a sustainable tempo. What that means is that the Development Team needs to be pushed to reasonable limits. Thus, you cannot expect the Development Team to be working 12 hours a day and maintain that kind of pace over extended amounts of time. Of course, there are times when such things may be needed.

Supposing that for some reason the project should fall behind schedule, the Development Team must work at the best pace possible while the Scrum Master and the Product Owner figure out the best way in which to improve tempo and make up for lost time.

Also, keep in mind that Agile does not allow for falling behind schedule. If anything, Agile seeks to deliver ahead of schedule. Though delivering ahead of schedule is not a priority, it is preferred over falling behind.

This is why both the Scrum Master and the Product Owner must consider that pushing the Development Team to the max might not be the best course of action as this could lead the team to burnout and create a lot more complications for the project than anticipated.

There is one other character that is not normally included in a regular Scrum team but can come into the picture if needed. This character is called an "Agile Coach." An Agile Coach, as the name states, is a coach who can guide Scrum team members in the proper application of Scrum principles and methodology. This coach can come in handy especially when teams are brand new to Scrum and haven't fully developed the practice they need. So, the Agile Coach can "correct" mistakes and make sure that the Development Team adheres to the specifications of a Scrum project.

The Agile Coach is an expert who has experience in all three tiers of the Scrum project management domain. Ideally, the Agile coach would have experience as a developer thus providing them with the necessary knowledge and understanding of what a typical Development Team goes through. The Agile Coach may come and go as needed or work full-time with the Development Team while they learn the ropes of the Scrum methodology.

What is a "Sprint"?

Earlier, we discussed the various phases of a project. These phases are the natural process by which the work breakdown takes place within a project. Consequently, each phase contemplates different activities which are generally interdependent. Therefore, you cannot move on from one phase to another without completing the requisite groundwork. What this implies is that Scrum teams need to have a clear understanding of how the tasks from one sprint are needed in order to build on to the next one.

Sprints take place during the execution phase of the project in which the work that is done is actually conducive to producing the final product. As such, the Development Team takes center stage during each sprint. The Scrum Master and Product Owner play a secondary, supporting role in which they are there to make sure that the Development Team has everything they need in order to get the job done.

41

During sprints, it is highly uncommon to see the Product Owner involved in the actual work being delivered unless it is absolutely necessary due to extemporaneous reasons. The leader who is in charge of making sure everything goes according to schedule is the Scrum Master.

Thus, the Scrum Master is the player that looks at where potential issues may arise and find proactive ways of addressing them if they can be addressed ahead of schedule. If issues happen to be unforeseen for whatever reason, then the Scrum Master must deal with them, usually in coordination with the Product Owner, in order to allow the Development Team to keep working.

The only case in which the Development Team should stop working is in the case of a catastrophic event that would render the entire project inoperable. Nevertheless, reaching a point such as this would be an extreme case that no one in their right mind would have been able to predict.

Notwithstanding, sprints generally last between 2 to 6 weeks with the average sprint length being 4 weeks or a month, give or take a day or two.

The reason for this particular sprint length is that 4 weeks seems to be the ideal time for Development Teams to actually produce results. If sprints are shorter, then it would be harder to produce accurate results while having longer sprints may lead to time being wasted.

Of course, given Scrum's adaptable nature, if a 4-week sprint is too short given the dynamic of the project, then the Scrum Master and Product Owner may choose to go for a longer sprint the next time around. If they feel that there was time left over, then more work could be incorporated into the next sprint as opposed to shortening the following one.

It should also be noted that sprints may vary in length throughout the entire project. So, you could have a shorter, 3-week sprint at the outset of the project and then have 5-week sprints at other points in the project. While this is possible, it is not recommended as it could upset the Development Team's tempo and rhythm. So, the ideal way to go would be to keep sprint lengths as even as possible.

Sprints are built on iteration. This means that sprints have a repetitive nature in which each sprint will have the same steps and procedures done. What this does is provide a certain level of predictability into how each sprint is conducted. Considering that Scrum plays in a highly unstable and uncertain environment, incorporating some measure of certainty is ideal for Development Teams to build around.

In the next chapter, we will get into even more detail on how each sprint works. The most important takeaway at this point lies in understanding that a sprint is the main scheduling tool that is used to plan the work to be carried out in a project.

The Project Charter

During a Scrum project, a Project Charter is created during the planning phase.

The negotiating and drafting of the Project Charter are the responsibility of the Product Owner. It is written well before any of the multiple components of the project are put into place. In fact, the Project Charter may be written before the Scrum Master and Development Team is put into place.

So, what is a "Project Charter"?

In traditional project management, a Project Charter would be the contract that the customer signs with the company that is going to carry out the project. As such, Scrum does not advocate for a contract in itself, but rather, a document that reads more like a Memorandum of Understanding in which all of the ground rules are laid out for the governance of the project.

Therefore, the Project Charter will contain everything pertaining to the duration of the project, the deliverables, acceptance criteria, payment details, and any other provisions which the stakeholders deem necessary and appropriate.

The Project Charter, in itself, is not a legally binding document. Rather, it is a document of good faith that enables all participants to have clear rules about how the project will be governed. This plays into one of the principles of Agile which espouses working software over complex documentation.

Now, there will more than likely be a need for formal, legally binding contracts. In that case, the Product Owner will seek the necessary legal counsel that will take care of drafting the contracts based on the Project Charter. While it is the responsibility of the Product Owner to draft the Project Charter, it is not the Product Owner's responsibility of drafting contracts unless they are licensed attorneys.

The Project Charter must then be approved by the customer or stakeholder(s) commissioning the project. Upon approval, the Project Charter comes into force and becomes the official document that will govern the entire project's development.

Since there is no official template that is used to draft a Project Charter, I recommend drafting it a like Memorandum of Understanding in which it is explicitly stated that all of the stakeholders in the project agree on the clauses contained in the document and commit to upholding them at all times. There must also be clauses added pertaining to conflict resolution. While you would not be expecting the conflict to occur, you do want to make sure that it is included so that all sides are covered in case there is ever any kind of dispute among the parties.

Finally, the Project Charter, as the law of the land, must be discussed among all members of the Project Team so that they are clear about what they are expected to do and how they must do it. The Product Owner may also craft mini charters outlining the role of each member of the Development Team. This can be a useful tool especially when there are cases of Development Team members unclear whether an activity exceeds their scope of responsibility or not.

User Stories

Another of the Product Owner's main responsibilities the development of the so-called "user stories."

A user story is a detailed description of the needs for each part of the project, to help the team come up with the most appropriate solution. As such, user stories are like putting a name and a face to who will actually benefit from the project.

Let's consider an example.

The main output of the project will be a mobile fitness app. The app will track health-related stats such as the number of steps, time at the gym, eating habits and so on. The project has kicked off with a Project Charter signed and approved.

The Product Owner is now in an information gathering phase in which the customer has expressed what they need but are not exactly sure what the final product will be like. In addition, they are not entirely sure of who their core consumers will be.

Therefore, it's up to the Product Owner to come up with a user story based on what the customer has specified. As such, the customer's specifications call for the app to be directed at young adults who work in a high-pace environment and don't have a lot of time and attention for fitness. So, the app is intended to provide reminders pertaining to drinking enough water, taking a break to stretch and so on.

With this in mind, the Product Owner can come up with a user story detailing who that specific user will be. Consequently, a user story can look something like this:

"Joe is a 28-year-old bank employee who typically works 12-hour days. He is single and lives with his dog in a one-bedroom apartment located in the downtown area of a large metropolitan city. He walks to work every day as his office is about 15 minutes away. He prefers to walk rather than take public transportation since the walk allows him to get exercise. He is health conscious but doesn't always have time to follow a strict diet. He is also very technologically inclined. He tries to use his smartphone for virtually everything he can."

This user story is just a sample. It could be even more detailed. In fact, the higher the level of detail, the better the context it will provide the Development Team in creating the app with these characteristics in mind. User stories can also be very specific to describe a feature, such as:

"*As a* user, *I want to* see how many steps I've taken each day and how that compares to previous days, *so that* I can track my physical activity, *in order to* lose weight."

Once the Product Owner has come up with this user story, the customer will have a look at it and request changes or sign off on it. Once the customer is happy with it, the Product Owner is now ready to get the ball rolling on the development of the app itself.

Now, there are a couple of twists here: The Product Owner could choose to do the entire user story process alone or choose to hire the Scrum Master in order to craft it together. Another option is where the Product Owner hires the entire Scrum team and develops the user stories as a collaborative team process. This is actually a good idea especially when the Product Owner does not have a great deal of expertise with the product being developed.

It should be noted that the Product Owner does not need to be an expert in the actual product being developed but does need to be an experienced Scrum practitioner. The Scrum Master should at least have a working knowledge of what the product is and what its development process is like. The ones who should be experts in the product being developed are the members of the Development Team.

One final note on user stories: user stories are based on real customers who will use the product once it's released. As such, the Product Owner may choose to talk to potential customers in order to get a feel for what they want. There could be focus group discussions, interviews and any other kind of research needed in order to gain the intelligence needed to create a viable user story.

Acceptance Criteria

Finally, the last component in a Scrum project is the acceptance criteria that the customer has outlined in order to determine the product's level of quality. If the acceptance criteria are not met, then the Scrum team must go back and figure out what's wrong. Though it should be noted that acceptance criteria are taken into account throughout the entire development process. Therefore, if the Development Team keeps these parameters in mind, there shouldn't be complications in actually achieving the acceptance criteria.

Acceptance criteria can come in the way of specific functionalities that the product provides. This can be written either as a checklist or as an extension of a user story. In the previous example, we talked about a fitness app. So, an example of acceptance criteria for this fitness app could be:

"*Given* I have walked 10,000 steps, *When* I hit this target, I get a notification through the app."

Other acceptance criteria could be automatic reminders for medication and vitamins. It may also include spoken alerts saying, "it's time to drink water." Of course, that is something that the customer would specify, and the Development Team must produce.

Now, it should also be noted that the Development Team should not produce anything that is not asked for. This means resisting the temptation to "improve" upon the customer's ideas.

Why?

Unsolicited features and functionalities may lead to useless work. The customer may not appreciate the added features or may even question why it was added in the first place. This can lead to wasted time and resources. Any "improvements" should be brought up the Development Team through the Scrum Master so that the Product Owner can speak to the customer and let them know what the Development Team wants to do and why they want to do it.

Once the customer is aware of what is going to be done and why it is needed, the Development Team can proceed with confidence. This is the type of ongoing communication that all sides need to maintain. Of course, since no one is perfect, there may be situations that were overlooked at the outset of the project, but which became apparent during the product's development. So, the Development Team can bring up their issues and concerns and let them be known.

Acceptance criteria are laid out in the Project Charter and can be listed as a checklist for the Development Team's benefit. With the user stories, acceptance criteria and the functionalities requested by the customer, the Development Team can work together to decide how they will achieve the acceptance criteria and produce the results.

Since Scrum teams are self-governing, the Development Team itself can decide how they want to approach the development of the product. The Scrum Master will only serve as a moderator throughout the process and take note of what is needed in order to get the job done.

The final details of the work to be done will be highlighted in the Scrum Burndown chart. The Scrum Master and especially the Product Owner, work on the sidelines ensuring that everything is going according to schedule.

In subsequent chapters, we will be going into very specific detail about what happens during a sprint and how each of the players interacts with one another. In addition, we will provide some practical examples that should help you to better understand the way Scrum projects are conducted in a typical, day-to-day environment.

Chapter 3: Sprints Within A Scrum Project

In this chapter, we will go deep into what a Scrum sprint is, how it works, and what elements make up a typical sprint. Also, we will be providing examples in addition to contrasting how a typical sprint stacks up against traditional project management processes.

Sprints within a Scrum project are essentially individual parts of the execution phase of a project. As stated earlier, the execution phase of the project is where the actual work is done. As such, it is where the products are developed, and the project's objectives are completed.

The initial sprint in a Scrum project begins when the Project Charter is approved by the customer, and the user stories are ready. Of course, the project team also needs to be in place in order for work to get started.

It should be noted that it's up to the Product Owner to determine how soon the project team will be put together. And there is no specific order in which the team should be put together. A traditional approach would be to have the Product Owner choose the Scrum Master and then the Product Owner and Scrum Master choose the Development Team in tandem.

However, this is not always the case. It could be that the Product Owner chooses the Development Team and then chooses a Scrum Master based on the Development Team. So, the Product Owner can choose the players on their team based on what the project is about and how it could be developed.

Let's look at a couple of examples of how a Scrum team can be put together.

First, let's assume that the project idea is born within a company, but the project team will be completely external from the company. Therefore, the company that is looking to put this project to work will be looking for an external consulting firm that can help them implement the project.

Now, this company is looking to implement a project for the improvement of a completely new employee benefits scheme. In this case, this is something the company has never done before. While it did have a traditional employee benefits scheme based on performance bonuses and holiday time, it is clear to the company directors that something a little more modern needs to be put into place.

So, the CEO of the company has received the Board's permission to go ahead and implement a new employee benefits scheme that revolves around a series of fringe benefits and other non-monetary incentives that can boost employee morale and thereby boost productivity.

Since the company is unsure about how to implement this project, the Human Resources department has indicated that since they are understaffed and behind on most of their work, they would rather only take a lesser consulting role.

As such, the company's directors have agreed to the hiring of an outside consultant who could oversee the implementation of the new employee benefits scheme. Since the time is at a premium, the Board is anxious to get the full system implemented in about 8 weeks. The reason for this time slot is because there are roughly two months left before the end of the current quarter. So, the directors feel that it would be great to get the new scheme in place right before the start of the new quarter.

The Human Resources manager has been tasked with finding the right person for the job. Through some recommendations, a great consultant was found. This consultant has ample experience in the restructuring of companies. So, this individual seemed like a good fit. And, this consultant is also a Scrum practitioner.

This consultant has met with the directors of the company, and they have all agreed that it would be best to bring in unbiased individuals from the outside. This would make it easier for the project team to make objective decisions since they don't have a personal stake in the company.

The first thing that the consultant has done is to take on the Product Owner role. This individual has decided that Scrum is the best way to go since there is no clear indication of how the new benefits scheme would work, and what the reactions of the company's current employees would be.

Therefore, the Product Owner has decided to get started by drafting up the Project Charter. This chapter contains all of the stipulations that will govern the life of the project. In addition, the consultant has had a lawyer draft up a legal contract in which all of the provisions contained in the Project Charter are officially signed and agreed upon.

Once the charter is signed, the company has agreed to give the consultant one week to get the project team together and kick off the project. Given this consultant's experience with projects in the past, the consultant has placed a few calls to some friends who might be interested in the Scrum Master's role. After a couple of calls, a qualified candidate has agreed to join the project.

The new Scrum Master has technical expertise in financial matters. In addition, these two individuals have worked together in the past. So, it makes sense that they join forces once more in this new endeavor.

The next step is to get the Development Team together. After some conversation and discussion, both the Product Owner and the Scrum Master have agreed that they need four members for the Development Team. They have decided what role each individual will play and what sort of expertise they need.

In this case, they have decided that they need four experienced individuals in the areas of Finance and Human Resources. Ideally, each candidate would have expertise in both areas, but they will settle if they have experience in just the one area. In any event, having two members with experience in Finance and two with experience in Human Resources would be acceptable too.

In addition, the payment terms in the Project Charter afford the hiring of four members of the Development Team, in addition to the compensation for the Product Owner and the Scrum Master. So, money also plays a role in determining the size of the team.

At this point, the Product Owner, Scrum Master, and the Development Team have all been assembled and are ready to get started working collaboratively. Their first order of business is to develop the user stories that will become part of the finished product that will be delivered to the customer.

The reason behind the Product Owner's decision to have the entire team work on the user stories is because the Development Team has ample experience in determining what would be good inputs for the new benefits scheme.

In order to get the user stories done quickly, the Product Owner has also decided to have one mega-meeting in which the entire project team would hammer out any, and all, user stories in one 8-hour session.

At the end of this session, and a couple of pizzas, three user stories came about.

The first user story is intended for the employees who have recently joined the company, that is, who have less than 1 year in the company. These employees make about roughly 20% of the company's workforce. So, they do represent a decent chunk of the payroll.

The second user story is intended for employees who have been with the company for over a year, but less than five years. These employees have enjoyed the company's previous benefit scheme but have also complained the most about it. As such, these are the employees who will be hit the hardest with the new changes that will occur. This group makes up over 50% of the workforce in the company.

The third user story is intended for those employees who have been with the company for over 5 years. This group makes up the remaining 30% of the workforce and represent a considerable amount of leadership positions within the company. They have also enjoyed the company's previous benefit scheme though it is unclear how they will react to the proposed changes.

Each user story has been drafted in such a way that every one of the groups highlighted has a name and a face that characterizes them. These were crafted out of the information the project team got from the company itself in addition to the project team's previous experience. With this, the project team is now set to work on the project and ready to make progress.

This is the first example I would like to provide you with on how to make up a Scrum team. As you can see, the entire team is external and foreign to the inner workings of the company. Consequently, they should be free to think outside the box and come up with novel solutions for the needs of this company.

Now, let's consider the second way in which the company could put together its project team based on a Scrum mentality.

The CEO got the green light from the Board on the project. The CEO has asked the Human Resources Manager to be the project lead. This was more an imposition than anything else. However, the company has offered the Human Resources Manager, as well as any other member in the company who participates in the project, a bonus for their work on this project.

Since the Human Resources manager has been trained in Scrum, they understand how the process works and are keen on delivering the best possible outcome for the customer.

After being officially notified of what the company's expectations are for the project, the Human Resources manager has decided to take on the role of Product Owner. This manager will be the main interlocutor between the CEO and the Development Team.

The next step is to find the Scrum Master.

The Product Owner has identified a colleague from the Finance department who is very knowledgeable about payroll and restructuring in addition to having an understanding of Scrum. After getting approval from the Finance Manager and the CEO, the Product Owner has a new Scrum Master.

Together, the Product Owner and the Scrum Master have come up with the Project Charter. The reason for doing this exercise like this is to cover all of the aspects which ought to govern the project. After a good morning's worth of work, the Project Charter is set. The CEO reads it, makes some observations, changes are made, and the Project Charter is officially in place.

Now it's time to put the Development Team together.

The Product Owner has convinced the CEO to let them pull four members from the various departments into the company as full-time developers. The CEO has reluctantly agreed to let them work on the project full-time for four weeks. So, that means that the Development Team has four weeks to put the entire plan together and produce the outputs the project intends to produce.

As such, this would only provide one month, or what could basically be just the one sprint.

So, the four employees chosen for the project were selected based on their experience, knowledge of Scrum and their dedication to the project. Since the CEO agreed to give an additional bonus to whoever took part in the project, the selected members of the Development Team seemed to be very motivated to get started.

With this, the Product Owner has its team in place.

However, since the Product Owner feels that the having the Development Team participate in creating the user stories is inappropriate due to their personal stake in the project (they will benefit from a new benefit scheme), the Product Owner has decided to create the user stories alone.

Once the user stories have been crafted and approved, the project is now officially set to get underway.

In this example, the Scrum team came from within the company. This means that the company won't have to pay an external consultant to do the job. Although, it does represent a cost to the company as they will be away from their usual jobs for the next four weeks.

Also, the Product Owner has the option of hiring an Agile Coach to guide them through the process of this new project. The Board has agreed to hire such a coach as this would enable the team to work out any questions they may have about Scrum or any other aspects which could be improved.

This example underscores a rather unconventional way in which a team can be put together. In total 6 employees were plucked away from their regular jobs. That is, the Product Owner, who is the Human Resources manager, still has their regular job to worry about. But since being a Product

Owner does not require full-time participation in the actual activities, it allows the Human Resources manager to carry on their work.

Of course, the Scrum Master and the development team are working full-time as they only have four weeks to get the job done. In addition, since Scrum calls for co-located teams, the Product Owner has given them a vacant office to use as a meeting room/war room where they can work together to get the job done. Thus, the project management is on the clock and must deliver the first results in the next couple of weeks.

The two, previous examples underscore the importance of having a solid Development Team that is eager to get started. They can come in and get started at any time while allowing the entire project team to feel comfortable about the work that is going to be done.

Getting That First Sprint off the Ground

In Scrum, there are a series of meetings which take place at various intervals. These meetings are what make the Scrum methodology work.

When the first sprint is set to get started, the project team will have what is called a "Sprint

Planning Meeting." In this meeting, the entire Scrum team will sit down and go over the work breakdown for the sprint, what to expect, and any concerns that are on the minds of the members. In addition, work is prioritized and estimated on the time needed for each of the activities. This is called "timeboxing," and it is a rigid standard by which all of the members of the team must adhere to.

At this point, the Sprint Planning Meeting is the only one which the Product Owner is required to attend until the end of the sprint. The Scrum Master should attend all meetings while the Development Team must be engaged in every single one of these meetings.

Once the work breakdown has been agreed upon, the sprint is set to begin. Ideally, it would begin on the first day of the work week, so there is a logical starting point to the sprint and conclude on the last workday of the workweek in which the project concludes.

Each of the members is now ready to get to work and begin carrying out the tasks they have agreed to. Bear in mind that Scrum teams are self-organizing. So, the team itself decides who does what, how long it should take, and how the end result of the tasks would be.

Every working day begins with the "Daily Standup Meeting." This meeting is done on a daily basis and is intended to provide every team member with the opportunity to voice any concerns, ask for help, request anything they might need and talk about what they expect to get done on that day.

This should last no more than 15 minutes. The Product Owner is not required to attend the Daily Standup Meeting, though the Scrum Master is most certainly required to attend. Each of the team members will have a chance to speak while the Scrum Master takes note of what is being discussed.

The Daily Standup Meeting also serves as a log of the items discussed and provides the Scrum Master with a registry of the thoughts expressed by the Development Team. This registry should provide insights into upcoming sprints and other projects.

In addition, the Scrum Master and Product Owner should have at least one weekly meeting in which all of these concerns are expressed. This will allow the Product Owner to brief the customer on the progress being while gaining perspective from the customer as to what the customer expects from the project.

Now, let's assume that the sprint lasted four weeks. So, at the end of the sprint, the "Sprint Review Meeting" is held. This meeting is essentially a demonstration that is provided to the stakeholders in the project so that they may see the advances that have been produced as part of the previous sprint. This is a good chance for the customer to provide any feedback, through the Product Owner, and which the Development Team can take into account while continuing to develop the final outputs of the project.

The Sprint Review Meeting is also the official ending of the sprint. With that, the Development Team is now ready to move on to the next sprint. While it is not recommended for there to be any kind of a break, the Product Owner and Scrum Master may agree to let them off for a long weekend just to let them disconnect from the project especially if the previous sprint had been demanding.

The next meeting that takes place is the "Sprint Retrospective Meeting."

In this meeting, the entire Scrum team is together. The Product Owner can provide the customer's feedback on the demonstrations conducted, while the Scrum Master can also go over any of the observations made during the sprint. Each of the Development Team members has the opportunity to express what they felt was done right and what they feel could be improved.

In addition, "mistakes" must be addressed at this meeting so that they can be "corrected" in the upcoming sprint. Also, the Product Owner and Scrum Master can go over any change requests the customer has made so that these changes may be incorporated in the next sprint.

As such, Scrum practitioners should note, especially Product Owners, that change requests from the customer should not be implemented mid-sprint. This may end up disrupting the tempo that the Development Team has achieved. This is why the Product Owner must be clear that with the sprint underway, it is very difficult to shift course and meet deadlines.

Consequently, any change requests should be implemented in the following sprint so that there is a logical break in the tempo of the work being conducted and the Development Team has a chance to plan how they will tackle that change.

The only reason change requests should be admitted mid-sprint is if there is some type of urgent need. This could be due to many factors. But the bottom line is that only a major event could trigger a change request mid-sprint.

Once the Sprint Retrospective Meeting is done, the Scrum team should move onto the next Sprint Planning Meeting. So, assuming that the Sprint Retrospective Meeting was conducted on a Friday afternoon, the next Sprint Planning Meeting can be conducted first thing Monday morning. Once the next Sprint Planning Meeting is in the books, then the next sprint may officially begin.

One question that often comes up: how many sprints should there be in a project?

The simple answer is that there need to be as many sprints as are required by the customer's request and the estimate on the time and work breakdown. Consequently, it's very difficult to say that each project should last two sprints or three sprints.

In the end, it all depends on the type of project you are working on and the type work to be done. This is why many Product Owners will have their team in place before committing to timelines. That way, they can be sure that the time estimate set is the best one based on the experience of the Development Team.

Scrum Artifacts

Do you recall the Agile principle that values working software over comprehensive documentation?

Well, Agile and Scrum do have some documentation which needs to be taken care of. The main difference is that the documentation generated in Scrum isn't as extensive as in other project management methodologies.

As such, there is a set of documentation which is generated that serves to keep a log of the actions that are done. The reason for keeping this log is to track and monitor the development of the tasks being done as they are completed throughout the course of a sprint. These logs then serve to provide stakeholders with information on the status of the project.

The Product Backlog

In short, the Product Backlog is everything that is going to be completed in a project.

Now, the Product Backlog should not be confused with the final output. The final output could be working software. So, the Product Backlog is all of the actions that need to be done in order to reach that final outcome.

The Product Backlog is the responsibility of the Product Owner. Although, it is recommended that the Product Backlog is built as part of a collaborative effort by the entire Scrum team. The reason for this is that the Development Team can estimate whether or not given tasks are really

69

needed. The evaluation on the part of the Development Team can determine if the tasks to be conducted make sense or if other tasks need to be implemented as well.

When the Product Backlog is created as part of a collaborative effort, the entire Scrum team can feel empowered because they had a say in the activities and tasks that are to make up the project. Also, it is quite possible that Development Team members have experience which they can put to good use during the project itself.

The Product Backlog can simply be a grocery list of tasks which need to be completed. The main thing to keep in mind, though, is that even if it's just a list, the interdependencies among the various tasks need to be established. This will allow for the Development Team to understand which tasks need to be done first in order to build on them and move onto subsequent tasks.

It's also worth noting that the Product Backlog should lead the Scrum team to determine which actions will happen in which sprints. Thus, the need for identifying interdependencies is crucial in developing a proper work breakdown structure, not just for each sprint, but for the entire project itself.

In addition, the Project Backlog will end up becoming the checklist by which the Scrum team will determine the progress being made.

The Sprint Backlog

Once the Product Backlog has been established, then the Sprint Backlog can be created. This backlog is a list of the tasks which will be completed in that given sprint. The Sprint Backlog is created at the Sprint Planning Meeting.

When the Sprint Backlog is created, the tasks that will be completed are created, and then they are assigned to the various team members. This provides a clear discipline as to who will tackle what, leading the team to have a clear understanding of what needs to be accomplished during that sprint.

It should be noted that the tasks chosen in a given sprint should lead toward providing the customer with a glimpse of what the final product will be especially in its early stages. While demonstrating fully functioning software during the first sprint may not always be possible, it is certainly possible to consider producing an advance that will enable the customer to see where the product is going.

Product Backlog Item

A Product Backlog item is a specific task that needs to be completed as part of the overall achievement of the project outcomes. Usually, each Product Backlog item is comprised of several smaller tasks which build up to it.

Now, one large Product Backlog item could become the focus on an entire sprint in which the smaller tasks are completed by each team member. Also, a Product Backlog item might be the sole responsibility of one team member. As such, the team member will perform tasks in each sprint leading up to the final implementation of that Product Backlog item.

One interesting comparison between Product Backlog items with traditional project management methodologies is that Product Backlog items would be considered to project objectives. As such, project objectives tend to have an overarching presence throughout the entire execution of the project. Consequently, it's important to keep in mind that Product Backlog items are more general and provide guidance to the tasks at hand.

Sprint Tasks

Sprint tasks are the individual tasks that are to be achieved during a sprint. These tasks have an important function in the development of the project as their achievement will lead to the overall construction of the final deliverables.

Sprint tasks can be individually assigned to specific developers or can be developed in tandem. The main point to keep in mind is that sprint tasks need to be completed during that sprint. They cannot carry over into subsequent sprints. If the team is unable to complete a task, for whatever reason, then this needs to be addressed at the Sprint Retrospective Meeting. It would also be part of the Scrum Master's job description to find a proper solution for it.

During the Sprint Planning Meeting, the Scrum team will decide which tasks will be included in that sprint and then proceed to time box it. The team must be clear on how long each task will take, what work needs to be done in order to achieve it, and how many members need to work on each task. Ideally, you could have one member per task though that may not always be possible.

This is the reason why the decision of what to include in each sprint needs to be a collaborative decision, taking the input from developers as the most important criteria. Unless developers are completely new to Scrum, they will have an idea of how to handle the workflow they are going to take on.

Sprint Burndown Chart

The Sprint Burndown Chart is a visual representation of the progress being made in throughout the sprint. As tasks move from one part of the chart to the next, the team can get a sense of how the project is coming along.

As such, the chart measures the amount of work already done versus the time left. In a perfect world, the trend line generated by the chart should have a downward trend at a 45° angle. If this is the case, then the sprint is right on schedule. If it is trending sideways, then there is no progress being made, while a vertical trend line means that all of the tasks have been completed at the same time. Of course, such a thing is not possible.

Other times, the trend line in a Sprint Burndown chart may look like stairs. That this, one flat line moving sideways, followed by a vertical drop, and then another line moving sideways. This trend is perfectly fine and shows clear evidence of progress.

The Sprint Burndown chart should be seen as the definitive measure of the Development Team's progress. Therefore, it should be updated by the Scrum Master as tasks get done and results are being seen.

Product Burndown Chart

The Product Burndown Chart is the main tracker of the tasks being completed. This chart tracks the completion of the Backlog items. In short, it is a tracker for the completion of each sprint. Therefore, this chart serves as a measure for the team to see how far along they are in the overall completion of the project. It also allows the customer to see how far the project has come along.

This chart is generally updated by the Scrum Master, though it could be updated by the Product Owner as a part of the normal course of action at the end of each sprint. Although, it is highly recommended that it should be updated each time a Product Backlog item is completed.

As with the Sprint Burndown Chart, the trend line will determine how the project is coming along. Once this chart has been completed, then the project is essentially over and ready for the final acceptance criteria to be met.

Final Thoughts

Well, that was quite a bit of information we dealt with. I know that this may be a lot to take in, but I assure you that if you go step by step, you will be able to get a very good grasp of how a sprint starts and ends.

So, it is important for you to have a clear definition of all the tasks to be completed as part of the overarching Product Backlog items and how these can be broken down into the smaller, more specific Sprint tasks.

As each sprint is completed, the entire Scrum team, as well as the customer, will be able to see the actual progress of the project and how it can be used as a means of demonstrating to the customer where the project is headed and how much there is left to go.

Bear in mind that the number of sprints in a project should be dictated by the work to be done itself and the time you have available to do it in. So, this is why the planning process, just like the entire project itself, should be a collaborative effort that fosters communication and leads to effective decisions based on everyone's collective experience and insight.

At the end of the day, the lifecycle of a Scrum project is based on the team's ability to stay on track. This is why the only truly rigid aspect of Scrum is the respect to the overall time allotted to each task. This discipline enables Scrum teams to meet their deadlines on a consistent basis.

Chapter 4: Roles in Scrum and Responsibilities

In the previous chapter, we talked about what a Scrum sprint is in great depth and how you put your first Scrum project together. In addition, we focused on the ins and outs of selecting your Scrum team. As such, this discussion was intended to get your mind working on how you can implement Scrum in your organization.

In this chapter, we will focus specifically on the roles contained within a Scrum project. We have already touched upon each one of these roles, though the time has come to be far more specific since each one of the players on a Scrum team has a specific role which they must fulfill. Furthermore, we will have a much closer look at what type of criteria will go into selecting each one of the team members.

Where to Find Qualified Players

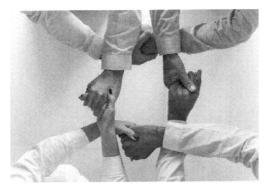

Finding qualified Scrum practitioners isn't as easy as you might think. While Scrum has gained considerable popularity in recent years, qualified Scrum practitioners aren't quite as easy to find. The reason for this is that there is still some lack of knowledge and understanding of the value of Scrum and project management as a whole.

Nevertheless, more and more companies are trying their best to recruit talent which has received some type of Scrum training. Also, companies may be looking to hire individuals who have taken Scrum training. This is especially true in the software and IT industries.

When you, and your organization, decide to go all-in on Scrum, it's often a good idea to build a culture of Scrum from within, that is, train current staff in the ways of Scrum. This can be a good way to foster team building and encourage your staff to work as a team in a collaborative manner. Most importantly, you're initiating the mindset transition from a traditional approach of doing business to a more Agile approach.

Thus, implementing Scrum in your organization leaves you with two options: either bringing in someone external who can get started with Scrum in your organization, or train your current staff in the ways of Agile. Please bear in mind that training your staff can be a way in which your organization can reward and motivate its staff in order to improve their skills and knowledge.

One way of training your staff without breaking the bank is through hiring an Agile Coach. An Agile Coach can help your staff learn the ways of Agile and Scrum in such a way that your organization and staff can shift their mindset to an Agile mindset.

The Agile Mindset

When an organization makes the decision to go Agile, the biggest challenge they face is shifting from a traditional mindset to an Agile one. This shift in mentality is a means of changing focus to a customer-centered approach in which embracing change is the primary focus.

This can prove to be both scary and even overwhelming to some folks.

Embracing change is not easy for many individuals and organizations. When organizations go down this road, individuals become closer-knit and more resilient. This resiliency makes organizations more adaptable and increasingly confident in operating within a dynamic environment.

In a way, an Agile mindset is about selling the idea to both staff and customers that change is to be embraced even when there is very little certainty about what might happen at the end of the project. While this approach does not imply improvising, it does mean that organizations need to think on their feet in order to produce the results that will get customers what they are looking to achieve.

That being said, Agile considers the following traits are prerequisites for Scrum practitioners:

- Positive attitude
- Willingness to learn
- Desire to serve others
- Provide value at all times
- Willingness to change
- Search for continuous improvement

While these characteristics are not exhaustive, they are some of the most common prerequisite characteristics that individuals need in order to embrace the Agile mindset. Of course, this isn't a cookie-cutter approach. However, the main aspect of this list is about making sure that potential Scrum practitioners have the willingness to embrace this change in mindset.

It should be noted that there are folks who may not be willing to embrace the Agile mindset. And they are in the right to choose to act the way they see fit. However, in order for Scrum to be effectively implemented, all team members need to be all-in in this mentality.

So, if you are looking to train your team, it's best to make sure that everyone is willing to go through the rigors that entail becoming a quality Scrum practitioner.

The Main Roles in Scrum

Throughout the book, we have highlighted the three main roles in Scrum: The Product Owner, Scrum Master, and Development Team. The actual number of players on a Scrum team will depend on the size and the scope of the project. Nevertheless, a standard project will require one Product Owner, one Scrum Master, and a Development Team that may consist of about 4 to 6 members.

It is not recommended to have a number greater than 6 members on a Development Team, nor is it advisable to have a number lower than 4. 4 members seems to be the ideal number as it is an even amount and provides the possibility of working in pairs.

If you happen to choose and odd-numbered Development Team, for instance, 5 members, there might be some discomfort since the team may not be able to break into pairs, or even may have difficulty in dividing up work. In addition, having an even-numbered Development Team provides asymmetry in the way the work can be divided and distributed.

Also, each Scrum project must have a Product Owner and Scrum Master. It is not recommended that to have one person play both roles as this could lead to a potential conflict in the way this individual may relate to both the customer and the Development Team. Since the Scrum Master's role is mostly about serving the Development Team, doubling up as a Product Owner may lead to one individual to be overloaded between the requests from both the customer and the Scrum Master.

In a way, the Product Owner should be on the customer's side. The reason for having this attitude is due to the fact that the Product Owner serves as a buffer between both the customer and the Development Team. This is why doubling up as Product Owner, and Scrum Master may lead this individual to take on too much especially if the project has a high degree of uncertainty and pressure due to time constraints.

With that being said, let's take a closer look at how each role plays out in greater detail.

Scrum Product Owner

The Scrum Product Owner is known as the "voice of the customer." As such, serving as the voice of the customer entails being on the "customer's side." What this means is that the Product Owner is the one who takes on the role of being a project lead without actually being the boss.

This is a very important shift considering that traditional project management methods espouse a "project manager" who is the boss and leader of the project. The project manager is the person who is responsible for the outcomes of the project but is also invested with all of the authority to make the project work.

In the case of the Product Owner, the Product Owner is not "the boss" since the Product Owner is in charge of making sure that all parties are working in unison. Considering that the Product Owner is not the boss of the project, the responsibility for the project's outcomes are not completely placed on the Product Owner's shoulders. This is a very important aspect to consider since the responsibility of the project can be distributed over the entire team and not just on one person.

Of course, if the responsibility for the project is distributed evenly among all members, then the credit for the project is also distributed evenly among all members. Therefore, the entire Scrum team needs to be on the same page. That is why all members of a Scrum team need to be willing to commit to this mindset. If there is any member that is not committed to this approach, then the project may encounter headwinds from within.

The Product Owner is the first member that should come on board for every new project.

But, where does the Product Owner come from?

Well, every project needs to have a project sponsor. The project sponsor is the main interested party in getting the project off the ground.

Earlier, I used the example of a company that is looking to change its benefits scheme. In that case, the CEO brought the need for a new benefit scheme to the Board of the company so that the project initiative may be authorized.

In this example, the CEO is the project sponsor as it was their initiative. Consequently, the CEO decided to ask the Human Resources Manager of the company to find a qualified individual who could act as a project lead. Since the project was conceived under the Agile framework, the project lead is not the Product Owner. The CEO continues to be the project sponsor while the Human Resources Manager, the person who hired the Product Owner, ends up becoming the customer.

So, why should the Human Resources Manager become the customer and not the CEO?

The CEO has a personal stake in this project. It was the CEO who advocated for the project to be done. This could entail a personal conviction for the project's realization. Therefore, the CEO would not be an objective party in the development of the project.

However, the Human Resources Manager may not have a personal stake in the project. This manager might be the one in charge of running the company's benefits scheme. So, they would be interested in making sure the project is done properly and also understands what the company's staff needs and demands from a good benefits scheme.

So, the Human Resources Manager becomes the customer while the Product Owner is now the focal point of the project. As such, the Product Owner is in charge of putting the project team together. This opens up an interesting point: the customer has no bearing on who is chosen to be on the Scrum team, though they may have some input as to the type of players they are looking from. After all, the customer is paying for the project. However, the customer needs to understand that their direct involvement in the project may end up doing more harm than good if it is not handled proactively and positively.

Ideally, the Product Owner should be an experienced Scrum practitioner even if they are not entirely familiar with the subject matter. The Scrum Product Owner needs to be a great negotiator and coordinator so that all of the activities which are carried out throughout the lifecycle of the project. Consequently, the Scrum Product Owner must be involved in the project from the beginning till the end even if the Product Owner is not directly involved in the actual development of the product.

One important word of caution for project sponsors: the first step toward launching any Scrum-based project is finding the Product Owner. Even if the project sponsor already has a potential team in place, the Product Owner needs to be in synch with the Scrum Master and Development Team. Therefore, choosing the Scrum Master or Development Team ahead of the Product Owner may lead to friction among all members. So, even if the project sponsor has people in mind, this decision may be discussed with the Product Owner, but it is the Product Owner's ultimate decision on who to include in the project team.

Also, if the project sponsor is bent on deciding who is on the team, then Scrum might not be the best approach. Since this attitude implies a more hierarchical approach, then a traditional project management approach may be more suited to this attitude. That way, the project sponsor can take the lead and let everyone else around them follow orders.

This is why Scrum is about working in a collaborative environment with a flat organizational structure. This breeds empowerment and allows Scrum team members to flex their muscles in search of a creative solution to the problems being addressed.

The Scrum Master

As I have stated earlier, the reason why the Scrum Master is called a "master" is not because of their domain over the team, but rather, it is due to their mastery of the Scrum methodology. This implies that the Scrum Master needs to be well-versed in Agile methodologies focusing specifically on Scrum. In addition, the Scrum Master should have a good level of knowledge on the project's subject matter. Therefore, the Scrum Master needs to be a well-rounded individual.

Unlike the Product Owner, who doesn't need to be well-versed in the project's subject matter, the Scrum Master needs to be involved in all technical aspects of the solution being required. The main reason for this is that the Scrum Master needs to clearly articulate the customer's vision, as expressed by the Product Owner, into the language that the Development Team can understand.

Since the Scrum Master is a subservient leader, their role is focused on helping the

Development Team get the most out of the resources they have available while maximizing the results obtained during each sprint. This means that the Scrum Master is not there to "lead" anybody, but rather, just be the figurehead which can provide the necessary guidance when the team requires it.

Bear in mind that the Development Team should be self-organizing. So, that means that the Development Team should be able to work out everything they need to work out on their own. However, there are times when the Development Team may need a referee to sort out the way things should be conducted. As such, the Scrum Master doesn't have to be "right" but should be able to provide proper guidance.

In the cases in which there is any type of dispute as to the proper application of Scrum methodology, then the final  decision falls on the Product Owner. It is the Product Owner who needs to provide proper guidance on the way the project is to be conducted. Again, this isn't about being right, but it's about having clear judgment as to how the methodology should be applied.

Moreover, the Scrum Master is in charge of making sure that the general guidelines of the sprint are being followed. For instance, the Scrum Master leads the Daily Standup Meeting and is in charge of going over the Sprint Burndown Chart. This is why it is required for the Scrum Master to be involved with the Development Team on a daily basis. While it isn't necessary for the Scrum Master to be sitting in the same room looking over everyone's shoulder to see what they are doing, it is a good idea for the Scrum Master to check in regularly to keep tabs on the work that is being done. The entire point of doing that is to make sure that if any potential issues arise, these can be caught in time.

The Scrum Master would ideally be someone who is experienced in Scrum while having a good working knowledge of the subject matter pertaining to the project.

So, assuming the previous example of the benefits scheme, the Scrum Master would not only be experienced in Scrum itself but would also have a working knowledge of payroll matters, compensation, benefits, finance, and any other applicable fields. As you can see, the Scrum Master is indeed a very well-rounded person that can provide insights into the actual subject matter but can also provide the necessary guidance to ensure that the project is conducted in the proper fashion.

If the Scrum Master isn't as experienced or is just starting out in this role, then the Product Owner may have to become more involved in working with the Scrum Master but not the Development Team. This would entail having more frequent meetings and phone calls just to check in with what's going on. In that regard, the Scrum Master may rely a lot more on the Product Owner for guidance and direction especially when there are methodological issues that need to be addressed.

In that regard, the Product Owner becomes a type of coach for the Scrum Master who then "coaches" the Development Team. However, when the Product Owner is under pressure, or may not be as experienced in the rigors of Scrum, then the project sponsor might consider bringing in an Agile Coach.

The Role of the Agile Coach

Earlier, we discussed who the Agile coach was and what they do within a Scrum project. As such, the Agile Coach is not a team member since the role of the Agile Coach is exists only when needed. What the Agile Coach does is provide definitive guidance on the way the project is to be conducted. Thus, the Agile Coach needs to be a veteran leader who has been involved with Scrum for a given period of time.

The Agile Coach can be an individual consultant, or perhaps a consultancy firm that provides these services. In the case that the Scrum team is comprised of members who work for the organization, then the Agile Coach needs to be external. This is important in ensuring the objectivity and impartial nature of the Agile Coach. If the Agile Coach is not objective, then what might happen is that an Agile Coach from within the organization may end up having a personal stake in the project. Therefore, this may lead to some bias in the way the project is applied.

In addition, an internal Agile Coach may be a bit reluctant to point out any shortcoming and inefficiencies out of concern for negatively affecting colleagues. As such, an independent Agile Coach can provide guidance and correct potential issues in the application of the methodology without really having to worry about stepping on any toes.

It should also be noted that the Agile Coach is not there to provide guidance on the way the project's outputs are being produced. In fact, the Agile Coach is limited to being a consultant in the project's methodology itself and not the product being produced.

So, let's assume that the Development Team has questions about the legality of a compensation scheme that they are working on. This would not be the competency of the Agile Coach, but rather, it would be the competency of legal counsel.

In that case, the Scrum Master may request the Product Owner to seek proper legal counsel and set up a meeting to discuss their questions. These consultations would ideally be coordinated by the Product Owner. Then, the Scrum Master may also be a part of the meetings in order to get the right idea on what the legal ramifications of the new compensation scheme would be.

After the consultation, the Scrum Master would go back to the Development Team and address any questions they may have. Since the Scrum Master has a working knowledge on the subject matter, they would be qualified to address the team on the subject. The Product Owner would just sit in the wings observing that the Scrum Master has a handle on the situation.

In the worst of cases, the Development Team may have to meet with the legal counsel in order to hear their opinion. While this may not be detrimental to the team in any way, it may temporarily put a halt to the team's work. That is why the ideal course of action would be to have the Scrum Master gain all the information needed while the team continues to work. As such, the Scrum Master's job, in this case, is in the background.

The Development Team

Last, but certainly not least, the Development Team is the main the component of the team. When the Product Owner and Scrum Master have agreed on all of the terms of the project, such as the Project Charter and user stories (unless being developed by the entire team), then the Development Team can be put into place.

Assuming that the team is entirely new, the Product Owner and the Scrum Master would have to make sure that they are qualified individuals who share the values of the Agile mindset. Now, if they have already worked in the past and have achieved a good degree of affinity, then much of this process would be reduced.

The members of the Development Team should all have had at least some training and exposure to Scrum while not necessarily being experts on Agile methodology. Ideally, they would be certified in Scrum development, though this may not necessarily be a deal breaker.

Members of the Development Team should also have a working knowledge of the subject matters on which the project is based. In the example of the benefits scheme, the Development Team could be a group of accountants who are experienced in compensations and benefits. Thus, a group of four accountants could be tasked with the development of the project.

For example, one individual might be in charge of going over the company's payroll history in order to determine the costs and benefits of the current benefits scheme. Another member might be in charge of putting together a list of viable benefits to be included in the new scheme. Another member might be in charge of calculating how much each of the individual benefits would save/cost the company while the fourth member of the team might be in charge of reviewing the company's balance sheet and cash flow statement to determine how much the company can reasonably spend.

As you can see, these activities all require technical knowledge in the field of accounting and finance. Since the Development Team members may not be very experienced with Scrum, the Scrum Master would be "holding their hand" at the beginning of the first sprint while the Development Team gains a good level of comfort with the way the project is to be conducted.

At the end of the first sprint, the deliverable from the Development Team could be a solid proposal for the company's Board to vote on. This proposal would contain a series of recommendations to be presented so that the directors can decide which benefits to keep and which ones would not be appropriate for their vision of the company.

Therefore, one of the acceptance criteria might be to have cost-effective benefits that the company doesn't have to actually pay out in monetary terms but could be offered to staff as a perk for working for the company.

Once the Board votes, they choose which initiatives to approve and which ones to axe. Then, the Product Owner meets with the Human Resources Manager and gets a series of change requests based on the appreciation of the company's Board. The Product Owner then talks with the Scrum Master to determine how these changes can affect the work already planned.

The change request is discussed at the next Sprint Planning Meeting. The Development Team can then get down to work and implement the final recommendations made by the board. As such, the second sprint would be to produce the final document which contains the company's new benefits scheme. This final draft of the document would constitute the final output of the project.

Then, the document is formally presented to the Board by means of a presentation conducted by the entire team. The Product Owner and Scrum Master are on hand to supervise what the Development Team has to say to the Board. The Human Resources Manager officially acts as the customer while the CEO and the Board are the relevant stakeholders.

The final draft is then approved, and the final product is officially accepted by the client. This marks the end of the project.

Do you recall that this project had 8 weeks to be completed? So, we decided to break it down into two, four-week sprints. And now, the project is officially at a close.

The remaining activities would be to have the Sprint Retrospect Meeting in which the entire team reflects on how the last sprint went and what could have been better.

Finally, there is a Project Retrospect Meeting in which the project is officially wrapped up. This meeting might end up being more social than work-related, but it is essential in order to bring the project to a formal close.

The Product Owner would be in charge of cleaning up the office after the Development Team has been disbanded and everyone goes their separate ways.

In the event that the members were part of the company itself, then they would go back to their usual jobs. In the case that the Development Team were all external consultants, then they would move on to other projects, either as a team or as individual members.

The Product Owner would be in charge of wrapping up the final details with the customer while the Scrum Master may still be on board for a bit longer in order to handle any loose ends with the documentation pertaining to the project.

With the conclusion of the project, the final deliverable is implemented by the customer and the story comes to an end.

Now, you might be asking yourself: wait a minute, what about the testing of the scheme?

Well, that is something that we are going to tackle in the next chapter.

Chapter 5: Metrics in Scrum

One of the core tenets of effective project management is producing metrics that can track the progress of a project. Without a solid, quantitative measurement of project performance, it is nearly impossible to accurately measure how effective the project actually is. In fact, offering a qualitative measure of the effectiveness of a project provides a very limited scope of just how well the project is doing.

Consequently, it is vital that project leaders develop a series of indicators which can be used to determine the progress of the project and verify how well the results of the project have been achieved. Based on that premise, Scrum, just like any other project management methodology out there, seeks to use indicators, formally known as Key

Performance Indicators (or KPIs) to measure the success of the project and track its output.

In this chapter, we will be looking at the KPIs which can be used to track project development in order to ensure that the outputs established at the outset of the project are met.

Who is in Charge of Tracking KPIs?

The first point that needs to be taken into consideration is: who is in charge of tracking KPIs?

The measurement of overall project success and progress is a collaborative effort, just like everything else in Scrum. The Product Owner is in charge of the overall reporting process, especially when reporting to the customer and other stakeholders on the progress of the project.

In addition, the Scrum Master is in charge of compiling the relevant information that is used to generate the indicators. For instance, this refers to tracking the results of individual Sprint Tasks which build up to the Product Backlog items.

The Development Team is also in charge of tracking their own progress such as the number of hours that have been worked and which are remaining in the sprint, the progress they have made in their individual tasks in addition to any bugs or problems encountered in the testing portion of the deliverables.

It should be noted that even if the Product Owner is in charge of compiling the KPIs for the project, this does not mean that the Product Owner has the authority to "supervise" the project. Please keep in mind that Scrum espouses a concept of transparency and mutual accountability. What this means is that everyone is in charge of tracking the progress of the project and not just the Product Owner.

Also, the Scrum Master is just keeping track of the tasks being completed in such a way that if there are issues that arise within the project itself, the Development Team has the opportunity to bring them up at the next available time which would be the Daily Standup Meeting.

Consequently, there is no officially tracker or supervisor. Everyone is in charge of keeping tabs on everyone. If there should ever be any disciplinary issues, the team, as a whole, has the responsibility and the authority to deal with the issue among themselves. This is one of the most important features of self-organizing teams.

Scrum Metrics and KPIs

The metrics used in Scrum are part of the broader group of Agile KPIs. These metrics serve as the parameters by which the progress of the project is measured in an objective and quantitative manner. Now, there are other metrics and methodologies which could come into play such as combining a Scrum project with Six Sigma or the use of Kanban metrics which track workflow.

The fact of the matter is that there is a wide range of metrics which could be used, and all depend on the project itself. As such, Scrum practitioners quickly come to realize that no two projects are the same and they may all end up requiring different metrics to measure their output.

Nevertheless, there are three broad types of metrics which can be used to generate KPIs.

• **Measuring deliverables**. These metrics measure the output of the Scrum team and the amount of value being provided to customers. This measurement can be in terms of time saved, cost reduction, increased sales, or any other type of impact the project has had on the customer. Also, deliverables may be measured in terms of their individual functionalities. This refers to the specific characteristics of the project and how it can be tracked to ensure that the final product does what it's supposed to do.

- **Measuring effectiveness**. These metrics measure the overall effectiveness and success of the Scrum team. There is a myriad of metrics here. Some that stand out are Return on Investment (ROI), time to market, and so on. These metrics focus on the impact that the Scrum team's actions had on the business itself, or even the industry.

- **Measuring the Scrum team**. These metrics look to determine the overall health of the team in terms of member satisfaction, turnover, and even attrition. This measurement allows the Scrum Master and Product Owner to determine if the way the project is being handled is appropriate if the tempo is moving too fast, or if there are any other considerations which must be taken into account.

The three broad categories of metrics described above are to provide a sense of what the Scrum team should be producing, where they stand in terms of the overall progress of the project and if there are any potential issues which could be caught ahead of time and dealt with in a proactive manner.

Therefore, it is up to the Product Owner to help the Scrum Master determine if the team is firing on all cylinders or if there are any issues within the team that need to be addressed at once.

In addition, it's important for the Product Owner to be aware of how metrics from other disciplines, such as Six Sigma, could potentially help the Development Team, and any other stakeholder, gain a better perspective of how well the project is doing. Ultimately, the success of the project is measured in the customer's satisfaction and the overall achievement of the project's aim. Moreover, the success of a project is measured by the amount of value that was ultimately delivered to the customer as a result of the deliverables.

Now, let's dig deeper into the specifics of each of the three broad categories we have described above.

Metrics Used to Measure Deliverables

This is the first category that we are going to take a look at. In it, you will find a series of metrics used to measure the overall success of the deliverables being provided to the customer. As such, the customers, as well as, all project stakeholders will have the opportunity to see just how well the deliverables are performing based on the project's individual characteristics.

These KPIs are a measure of how well the Scrum team has been able to deliver value to its customers and thereby accomplish the aims of the project. This measure of customer satisfaction enables the Scrum team to see if they are heading in the right direction, or if there is a need to make adjustments.

It should also be noted that since there is always partial delivery of outputs, it is possible to see how outputs are performing at the end of each sprint. This will enable the Scrum team to make any adjustments based on the feedback received during the Sprint Review Meeting.

Sprint Goal Success

The Sprint Goal Success is an Agile metric adapted specifically to fit the Scrum framework. This metric enables the Scrum team to determine if the overall result of the sprint was successful. In order to generate this metric, three basic questions need to be answered:

- What is the point of the sprint?
- What can we do to achieve the sprint goal?
- How can we tell we have achieved the goal?

The answers to these three questions should be able to guide you in determining if the overall result of the sprint was successful, or not.

So, the first question, "what is the point of the sprint?" refers to the sprint's main objective, that is, what is the overall goal of the sprint?

The answer could be something as simple as, "provide a functioning demo version of the software." This means that at the end of the sprint, the Scrum team should be able to have a fully-functioning demo version for the customer to evaluate.

The second question, "what can we do to achieve the sprint goal?" refers to the actions and resources that need to be combined in order to determine if the goal is reachable, or not. These goals can be taken from the Product Backlog and put into practice in each sprint through the Sprint tasks determined at the outset of the sprint during the Sprint Planning Meeting.

The third question, "how can we tell we have achieved the goal?" refers to finding an objective measure that can determine if the goal was met. If it was, then the Sprint Retrospective Meeting can capture the successful actions implemented. If the goal was partially met, or if the team failed to meet, then the very same Sprint Retrospective Meeting can be used to determine what went wrong and how it can be improved.

Ultimately, the criteria which can be used to determine if the sprint has been successful to compare the outputs based on the acceptance criteria. If the outputs comply with the acceptance criteria, then there is a good chance the customer will be satisfied even if the request changes. However, if the acceptance criteria are not reflected in the output, then the Development Team needs to go back and see how they can get back up to speed.

Escaped Defects

This metric tracks the number of bugs that the Development Team encountered during the development of the product. This particular metric is ideal for tracking those products which are reliant on testing in order to make sure it works well.

This metric can be used in manufacturing, software development, pharma, and even food production. If you look at it those terms, you can put Scrum to use in any field in which defects are tracked. The big difference between Scrum and other manufacturing systems such as Total Quality is that you are not waiting till the end of the production cycle to see where the defects are. With Scrum, you can gauge how many errors are popping during the manufacturing phase. Therefore, you will be able to determine if there are corrections that need to be made.

Defect Density

And, on the subject of defects, the Defect Density metric measures how many defects were found per unit of production. In the case of software, for instance, you could track the number of mistakes per lines of code. In manufacturing, you could track the number of mistakes per thousand units of production. The measurements may vary, but the concept is the same. As such, it's important to keep track of this measurement as it is vital to ensure that you have the right number of defects.

Team Velocity

This is a more Scrum-like measure. In essence, team velocity is measured by the number of user stories completed in a sprint, or the amount of Product Backlog items finalized.

Now, this metric is not an exact metric in the sense that some sprints may yield the completion of a significant number of products while other sprints may produce a very limited number. This all depends on the actual work breakdown that has been determined at the outset of the sprint.

Nevertheless, it is a useful measurement in tracking the actual work that the Development Team is achieving per sprint. However, it might be unfair to compare one sprint with another since conditions may be changing and the dynamics of the project may require one set of tasks over another. Thus, this may lead the team to produce a high number of outputs in one sprint while the remaining number of sprints may yield a lower amount of outputs.

At the end of the day, the team serves as a means of tracking the amount of work being done. As the completed work piles up, the Scrum team can see the success of their actions.

A word of caution though: in the case where there are multiple Scrum teams, it's important to avoid the sure of team velocity as a means of comparing team performance. Unless you have multiple teams completing the exact same tasks (which would be pointless) you would not have an "apples to apples" comparison. This means that while one team is apparently getting more work done than other teams, this measurement is not fair since each team is working on completely different tasks. As such, this is a flawed metric in terms of using it as a comparison among teams.

Sprint Burndown

The Sprint Burndown is a measure in which the sprint's total working hours are divided by the number of work days available.

Let's assume that a Scrum team has four weeks to complete a sprint. Then, let's assume they are working 8 hours a day over a 5-day week, that's 20 work days at a clip of 160 total hours of work.

This means that each day, 8 hours will tick off the Burndown Chart. If the team is humming along, there may be no need to work overtime. However, it could be that the Development Team has encountered issues and needs to put in a few extra hours. This would be reflected in the number of hours the team is working on a daily basis.

Consequently, you can chart the team's work by generating a bar graph representing the number of hours worked per day. The trend line for the chart would gradually wind down to zero as the number of hours run out.

The Sprint Burndown Chart serves as a graphic organizer in which the team can see where they are heading in terms of the remaining hours in the sprint versus the amount of work remaining. It should be said that if everything is humming along perfectly and the work assigned to that sprint takes less time than anticipated, the leftover time is automatically assigned to testing. That way, no time is wasted.

Measuring Effectiveness

The next set of metrics are used to measure how successful the Scrum team has been in achieving the business goals set forth the outset of the project and in each sprint. Thus, the Scrum team can see how effective they have been in generating value to the customer and to the team itself.

Time to Market

This metric tracks the amount of time the Scrum project actually takes before the product begins to generate income for the customer. So, this would be the number of sprints it would take the Scrum team before the final product is officially released and begins to generate income for the customer.

Let's consider a software release such as a video game. The Scrum team has determined that it would take four, four-week sprints before the Scrum team would have a demo version available for testing. At this point, the game would not be up for sale yet, but the advance speculation would provide the customer with some traction. As such, value is being created without actually being up for sale.

When the video game is fully operational and ready to generate income, then the Scrum team will have the final release of the product to the customer. At this point, the customer can begin to generate income off the product's final release.

This measure is also depending on the Scrum team's alpha and beta testing procedures. It could be that beta testing may take up an entire sprint since the product itself is so extensive. And once beta testing is complete, the product may enter the market under alpha testing guidelines. As such, this may represent another full sprint while the final bugs are worked out for the product.

As you can see, time to market becomes more and more critical as the project grows in size and scope. Therefore, it's crucial for the Scrum team to set realistic timelines so that the customer can be aware of the amount of the time the project will need before the final product is released.

Return on Investment (ROI)

This metric can be used on both sides of the ball.

For the Scrum team, their work generates an income to the company which has employed them to deliver the service to the customer. As such, the ROI for the company employing the Scrum team may be measured in terms of the costs associated with each sprint versus what the customer has actually paid for the services rendered.

This is fairly straightforward, and the Scrum team would most likely generate costs in terms of wages, equipment, and other materials used to produce the final product for the customer. Since the Scrum team may be employed by a company external to the customer, this external company, perhaps a consulting firm would have to make an upfront investment in equipment and training in order to get the Scrum team fully operational.

On the customer's side, the customer will measure the expense that arose from the actual payment of the services rendered by the Scrum team. This payment could be calculated and agreed upon in a number of ways. At the end of the day, the customer hopes to generate much more income as compared to the expense it incurred in during the production of the project's outputs.

The easiest way to breakdown costing for a Scrum project is per sprint. Since each sprint may have very different activities attached to them, the Scrum team may reduce or increase costs depending on the actions that are done.

Ultimately, the Product Owner and Scrum Master need to keep close track of the expenses incurred by the Development Team. In traditional project management approaches, one of the key elements in the planning phase is the development of a project budget.

In Scrum, since less documentation is favored, the Product Owner should be encouraged to have a means of tracking expenses such as a solid spreadsheet, which can keep tabs on the money being spent on project-related items. The worst thing that a project team can do is completely disregard their costs. So, it certainly pays to keep track of this metric.

Capital Redeployment

This is a very tricky subject.

At the outset of the project, the Product Owner needs to determine what capital equipment is going to be needed in order to carry out the tasks needed to produce the final output for the project.

In that regard, the Product Owner needs to see if the current capital equipment, such as computers, machines, or any other type of equipment can handle the demands of the project. Otherwise, the Scrum team may need to invest in new equipment in order to get the job done effectively. When there are acquisitions in capital equipment at the outset of the project, this is called "capital deployment."

However, what happens if there is a need to acquire more equipment mid-way through the project?

This is the case of "capital redeployment."

One consideration might be the acquisition of new equipment. Since it is likely that the new equipment may not be fully used up by the end of the project, it could still serve for a future project. Nevertheless, the cost of the equipment needs to be contrasted versus the reaming work to be done. When the cost of the new equipment exceeds the economic value remaining in the project, then this situation of "capital redeployment" makes no sense for the Scrum team.

Consider this situation:

About 60% of the project has already been completed. Consequently, the customer has already paid more than half of their share in the project. With about 40% of the work remaining, the Scrum team has determined that there is the need to acquire new computer systems in order to finish the remaining amount of work.

Now, for the sake of simplicity, let's assume that the customer owes the Scrum team $1,000. The cost of the brand-new equipment is $750. The Product Owner has determined that this would essentially zap any profits the Scrum team could make. Therefore, another option needs to be considered.

In the end, the Product Owner has decided that refurbished equipment would be more suitable given the amount of time remaining in the project. Consequently, the acquisition of brand-new equipment does not make sense for the Scrum team. Such a situation may have been avoided in a carefully-planned project, but there are always unforeseen events. For instance, the customer has put in change requests that forced the Scrum team to expand the scope of the project and hire new developers. So, it is certainly worth taking this into consideration.

Customer Satisfaction

The Scrum team's biggest concern is having a satisfied customer. Now, in the case of a project, customer satisfaction essentially means that the guy who's paying needs to be happy with the product and not the actual users.

Nevertheless, it's important for the Scrum team to track what the users have to say about the product. In this case, customer satisfaction can be measured during the beta testing phase. For instance, beta testers can fill out a short questionnaire following their experience with the product.

This questionnaire can have easily measurable metrics such as "like," star ratings, recommendations, or even abstract measurements such as asking users how much they would be willing to pay for a product such as this one.

Once the product is released, the Scrum team, most notably the Product Owner, may choose to hold some type of customer satisfaction review. This would enable the project stakeholders to determine how well the product met the expectations of the customer and the users. They may lead to another project in which bugs and kinks are worked out, or an alpha testing sprint that would officially bring the project to a close even after the product has reached the hands of the users.

Customer satisfaction can be contrasted with metrics such as ROI in order to visualize just how effective the project was in the end. Ultimately, this measurement would provide the stakeholders with a clear vision of what the product is able to do moving forward.

Monitoring the Scrum Team

These metrics are used to gauge the health of the Scrum team.

At the outset of this book, we mentioned how important people were over processes and equipment. And it goes without saying that the most important people in a Scrum project are the members of the Development Team. Without them, none of the work would be possible to do no matter how intelligent and talented the Product Owner and Scrum Master may be.

So, these metrics can be used to track the overall performance of the team and determine how well they are doing as a team, independent of their outputs.

Using Meetings to Gauge Health

The Daily Standup Meetings and the Sprint Retrospective Meetings are used to reflect on the daily tasks being conducted, as well as, the tasks achieved during the previous sprint.

It is during these meetings that the Product Owner and the Scrum Master can see just how well the team is performing. These meetings are a great way for the Scrum Master to pick up on potential issues within the team itself. Perhaps the team is encountering a difficulty which can be addressed early and well before it festers into something completely detrimental to the Scrum team's performance.

Also, the Scrum Master may pick up on potential issues which the Product Owner can bring up with the customer in order to figure out how to proactively deal with them. As such, meetings should be productive in such a way that the Development Team can use that time to generate the information that the Scrum Master and the Product Owner will need in order to fine-tune the processes being put into place.

Furthermore, the Scrum team needs to maintain open lines of communication at all time. Therefore, the Scrum team needs to be able to address issues within the team, given its self-organizing nature, without having to resort to additional intervention from the Scrum Master or the Product Owner.

Team Satisfaction

This is a hard one to track.

On the one hand, you could take your team member's word for it and take their comments at face value. So, if they say they are doing well, you could take that a face value and decide they are feeling fine. Likewise, if the team says things are not going well, you can take that at face value and determine what needs to be done in order to avoid future issues.

Now, you could find a more systematic approach, such as a reporting system in which team members can track how they feel on a daily basis by depositing smiley or sad faces in a box before they go home for the day. The Scrum Master can see how many smiley or sad faces are deposited at the end of each day. Since this is a perfectly anonymous task, Development Team members may feel compelled to be honest. Of course, there will come a time when they will have to indicate what's getting to them. But that can be part of one-on-one talks between the Scrum Master and individual team members.

It should be noted that satisfaction is something subjective. And, most Development Team members may simply feel overwhelmed by the tempo of the project or may feel uncomfortable especially if they are new to Scrum. So, encouraging constant communication at all times is vital to a healthy project.

Staff Turnover

We briefly touched on this subject earlier. There is a very real possibility that you may have to find replacements for team members mid-sprint. Of course, you would like to have a situation in which team members don't flake out in the middle of a sprint, but if it does happen, then you would be hard pressed to find a replacement.

Some Scrum teams like to have a "bench." This would mean a five-member squad when, in reality, four members are needed. But the fifth member is there to replace anyone who leaves. That will allow the team to cope with the work remaining as opposed to having a four-member team and the suddenly being shorthanded with three or even two members.

Turnover is a measure of how well the team is feeling. So, if you have a higher rate of turnover, then the team is not feeling well. If there is little turnover, then you can feel confident that the Development Team is doing just fine.

Final Considerations

When looking at metrics in a Scrum project, you must have a clear vision of which elements you can track objectively, and which ones would be tracked in a more subjective manner. Ideally, you would be able to track everything with statistical and numerical data in such a way that you could generate reliable numbers.

As such, great care needs to be taken in avoiding the use of the wrong type of metrics. When the wrong metrics are used, the information obtained may be misleading and thereby cause you to make inappropriate decisions. So, it certainly pays to do your homework on what metrics you could use in order to keep adequate track of your project.

I would greatly encourage you to look at comparable projects, whenever possible, to see which metrics you put into practice so that you can get a better understanding of how you can measure your team's performance.

Furthermore, using the right metrics to measure customer satisfaction will enable you to determine how effective the project was. At the end of the day, customer satisfaction is the ultimate measure of success for any Scrum project.

Chapter 6: Applications of Scrum

We are beginning to come to the stretch drive of this book. But there is still lots more to discuss.

In this chapter, we will be looking at the applications of Scrum. That is, we will be discussing how and where Scrum can be applied. This will give you a broader perspective on how Scrum is not just limited to software development. Since Scrum has cross-cutting applications, it's definitely worth jumping into a deeper discussion on how Scrum can be applied to your organization.

Born out of Software Development

When Agile was developed, traditional project management methodologies had been unable to address the issues pertaining to dynamic and ever-changing environments. This led project managers to seek alternatives that would embrace change and help software developers find the right way in which they could address these dynamics while making the most out of the current project management techniques available.

Out of this need, approaches such as Extreme Programming allowed developers to find a host of principles which could better address the circumstances they face as developers in a volatility environment.

Since 2001, the Agile movement has led to the emergence of Scrum as a viable methodology which can provide developers a series of steps and procedures in order to create a project framework conducive to getting results.

Given that we have already covered the history of Scrum; it's worth mentioning at this point that the software industry is the most common place where Scrum can be found in action. But it is not the only place in which Scrum can be implemented. In fact, Scrum can be implemented in any type of industry and business.

It Starts with the Agile Mindset

Throughout the book, we have talked about the Agile mindset.

In that regard, the Agile mindset is all about putting people first. In this case, the people that go first are the customer and the individual team members.

When you move away from getting results based on the cold metrics that are just numbers on a page to an approach where success is measured by the success of individuals, then you are setting yourself up for a successful run at each project.

One of the most crucial success factors in Scrum is determining if team members have the right mindset. This may imply having to "sell" individuals on the merits of Scrum especially if they have been exposed to other project management methodologies which espouse more rigid principles.

The fact of the matter is that anyone who is truly dedicated to providing the best value at all times will quickly see the merits of Scrum for what they are. As long as team members are willing to focus on delivering value at all times, and not just "getting the job done," then you can be sure that you will be successful in the long run.

A Cross-Cutting Approach

Scrum has a cross-cutting approach in the sense that it can be applied to virtually any industry and business out there. This is something which is important to take into account as project management is a diverse field.

Given that there is no, one methodology which is "perfect," new approaches are consistently being developed. As such, each approach attempts to tackle the gaps that other approaches have failed to address, either due to obsolescence or due to inadequacy on the part of their practitioners.

In any event, Scrum can be implemented in just about every walk of life. Increasingly, more and more industries are getting their staff Scrum certified so that they can tackle project management, and daily tasks, within an Agile environment.

Consequently, being "Agile" means being able to trim away the fat from your organization and focusing on getting results rather than sounding smart. In fact, you will sound even smarter when you are able to deliver on your promises as opposed to having to justify your team as to why your objectives were not met.

In this regard, you have the power to choose Scrum as a means of bringing your team into a more dynamic approach which can allow you to become faster, quicker and even get ahead of the game especially during times of uncertainty.

From pharma to manufacturing to business process outsourcing, Scrum has gained more and more traction as Scrum practitioners have been able to make headway in the application of Scrum to various facets of the business world. This is something which should not be taken lightly as most organizations are in a constant search for improving their processes in such a way that they can reduce both time and cost.

That being said, it's important to take into account that Scrum is just one of the methodologies under the Agile umbrella. Thus, you have a myriad of options which you can also check out. By learning more and more about Agile, you can see just how beneficial being Agile really is.

Other Methodologies to Consider

If you are serious about going Agile, I will encourage you to check out other methodologies which can help you get the most out of your Agile mindset.

The first is Lean Manufacturing.

This methodology is focused on trimming down the fat as much as possible during manufacturing processes. Lean Manufacturing is all about reducing errors while maximizing output. Often, this is achieved through the streamlining of processes which aren't always the most efficient.

In Lean Manufacturing, the idea of "time is money" is really taken to heart.

When you become "lean," what you are essentially doing is reducing the "waste" from your processes. So, this waste can be seen as a waste of time, a waste of money and even a waste of staff. Often, businesses will hire more people than they really need. Also, they will spend a lot more time on tasks which can be done in a reduced period of time.

Now, we are not talking about firing your staff and hiring a bunch of robots to do their job.

Hardly.

What we are advocating is for having the right amount of people, within the properly designed processes, which can yield more efficient results. Consequently, efficiency will lead to better profit margins and improved revenues for companies.

Becoming lean is all about embracing an out-of-the-box approach in which you are willing to consider different angles on processes which you might be considered to have down cold. But it's when you begin thinking outside of the box that true progress is made.

Also, becoming lean is a mindset, just like Agile, in which you are looking to maximize your uptime. As you become leaner, your uptime will yield more. Hence, you will be able to take advantage of the savings obtained in term of time and resources.

A great complement to Lean Manufacturing is Six Sigma.

Six Sigma is a methodology which tracks defects and attempts to find the best ways to reduce them. So, the first step for Six Sigma practitioners is to identify the number of defects that make up the entire manufacturing process.

Six Sigma is an ideal complement to Scrum since both Six Sigma, and Scrum seeks to find the best ways to produce given the circumstances you are dealing with. In that regard, keeping a mature attitude about the reality of a company is ideal in order to make the most of any restructuring process.

Therefore, Six Sigma seeks to encourage management teams to find ways to reduce the incidence of defects. This ties into the metrics in Scrum looking to measure defects in lines of code, for instance.

As I have pointed out throughout this book, the spirit driving Scrum is continuous improvement. That is the same attitude that drives Six Sigma. As such, Six Sigma will enable you to quantify your defects in such a way that you can see where you stand, and then, make a concerted effort to improve the overall quality of your manufacturing process.

So, I would encourage you to check out these the methodology mentioned herein. They will help you find additional elements which can help you improve your overall processes in such a way that you can ensure continuous development across the lifecycle of projects, as well as, your organization's daily tasks.

As such, keeping an open mind will be just as useful to you, and your organization, as any high-priced training seminar or course you can take. Bear in mind that investing in yourself, and your team, will always be beneficial insofar as ensuring consistent results as delivered to your customers and stakeholders.

Stacking Scrum up to traditional project management methodologies

Since Scrum is relatively new on the project management scene, the more traditional project management methodologies have become increasingly scrutinized in the way they handle many of the functions associated with projecting management.

It is worth noting that the comparison that we will make in this section is not about selling Scrum as a superior means of project management. If anything, both Agile and traditional project management share many common traits.

However, it is their differences which seem to generate some controversy among advocates and practitioners of the various project management methodologies. So, I would like to point out that is it important for you to become well acquainted with the various approaches out there. When you become familiar with the myriad of the project management approaches out there, you will be able to come up with a list of items which you can confidently apply to your own project management style, as well as, helping your team rally around what you feel to be the most effective means of carrying out projects.

Since Agile, and consequently Scrum, advocates for a flat hierarchical structure, all Scrum team members have an equal say in what is done and how it is done. This is a fundamental shift from traditional project management as a traditional approached call for a hierarchical structure in which the project manager reigns supreme.

While we have clearly established this difference earlier on, it's important to consider how traditional project management is heavy on a single point of accountability. Needless to say, this may become overwhelming to that individual who must bear the responsibility for an entire project.

That being said, it is important to consider how empowerment plays a key role in providing project teams the opportunity to do things as they see fit given the fact that it is the team members who are tasked with delivering the actual value at the end of the project.

Furthermore, traditional project management considers processes as the most important elements within a project. As such, we have stated how people are more important than processes. Of course, even the most talented individuals need to have clear processes and procedures on which they can rely on. Nevertheless, when greater emphasis is placed on processes over people, then the talents of individual team members may become stifled.

Hence, it is important to foster empowerment among team members. This can be achieved by allowing team members to use their criteria, judgment, and common sense to dictate the way in which they will approach the tasks they are to complete.

This is another fundamental shift in mindset as the more individual team members are allowed to think for themselves; the lesser the burden becomes to project leaders. This is why traditional project management approaches rely so heavily on project managers. In the end, it's the project manager who bears the burden of everything that goes wrong.

Yet, if the project runs smoothly and everything comes up roses, then it's the project manager who can claim credit for everything that happened in the project. This is another fundamental shift in mindset when dealing with Scrum. If the project is a success, then the entire team takes credit for it. In a way, it's like team sports that do not rely on one player to make the difference.

Think of Rugby.

In Rugby, one player cannot be a difference-maker. One player can come to a deciding factor, but one player is not enough to win a match singlehandedly. This is where the term "Scrum" comes from. It comes from Rugby; a true team sport in every sense of the word.

This is why the collaborative nature of Scrum is at the root of the way everything is done. If Scrum practitioners truly embrace the way of this collaborative nature, then there is a good chance that the projects you embark upon will be successful.

As for traditional project management methodologies, a more segregated, differentiated division of labor is espoused. The intent behind this division of labor is to foster specialization among team members in such a way that each individual will be in their area of expertise and thereby producing results.

While this logic makes all the sense in the world, it leads to communication breakdown and even competition among the various components of the project team. So, the project manager is often a mediator among the different sections of the project. Undoubtedly, this represents additional tasks which may not be really necessary. This is not a good example of being "lean."

How to Deal with Resistance

The last topic I would like to address in this chapter is resistance.

Often, Scrum practitioners encounter resistance, especially with those folks who are unfamiliar with the principles that Agile holds true.

This resistance is mainly due to the fact that any time you ask individuals to change their ways of doing things and even approach life, you will encounter resistance. Given that this is a perfectly natural response by a human being, it is also important to consider that not everyone is open to embracing the Agile mindset.

In that sense, there are folks who would rather not be a part of Agile processes and moving away from what they know best. As such, some folks believe that advocating for the implementation of Agile methodologies is about replacing previous ideas and beliefs since Scrum is somehow much better than other methodologies

As I have stated earlier, Scrum is not "better" than other project management methodologies. It is just "better-suited" for some types of projects and industries. This is a key difference since not all projects are created equal, and certainly not all fields have the same characteristics.

This is why Scrum's cross-cutting appeal is so useful. Nevertheless, making the most of the talent and resources available is a must for all project managers. Thus, being able to communicate the benefits of Scrum to team members is a valuable first step on the road to becoming Agile.

As you traverse through the paths of becoming Agile, your team members may bring up objections as to why Agile approaches and Scrum are not the best way to go.

One of the most common issues raised by folks is the lack of a hierarchical structure.

Since hierarchy is something that is deeply rooted in the psyche of all humans, it may be hard for some folks to wrap their mind around the fact that there isn't a boss, but rather, it is a team of "bosses" that runs the project.

In addition, some folks may resist that implementing Scrum usually requires some type of retraining or courses to be taken. As such, resistance can certainly be strong especially among older folks who may not be too keen on taking courses or go through retraining efforts.

However, it is certainly worth making the most of your time to learn more about how Scrum can have a direct impact on the way that you work and how your organization can benefit from going Agile. Moreover, teams that embrace Scrum are often closer and yield better results.

As individuals begin to see the ways in which Scrum can be implemented in a positive way, the Agile mindset will begin to take hold within your organization's culture. Eventually, Scrum and Agile will become second nature to an extent whereby everything will revolve around this newfound culture.

So, I would certainly encourage you to motivate your staff to take a closer look at how Scrum and Agile can help them become a much better team. Since Agile is all about continuous improvement, then the first important concept to embrace is exactly that: continuous improvement.

As such, continuous improvement begins with individuals within your organization becoming committed to continuously improve processes, outputs, and most importantly, themselves.

Therefore, approaching continuous improvement and development should become the norm among all team members.

That being said, your organization will soon become a breeding ground for success as team members become more and more aware of the need to help each other improve. This is something that I cannot stress enough: the collaborative nature of Agile. Without it, the entire building comes crashing down.

Also, collaboration breeds trust among team members. The more team members can learn to trust each other, the more they will be willing to take on the roles and responsibilities that Agile asks of them. Moreover, when teammates really trust each other, they will develop keen instincts in which they will be able to sense everything that is going on around.

This is just like sports. When teammates truly know each other perfectly, they can produce those "no-look passes" simply because they know where their teammates are going to be. Thus, this connection among teammates can lead to producing results on a consistent basis.

Finally, I would like to underscore the importance that leadership has on a successful team. When the leadership of a team is able to provide an example of consistency and dedication, that is something which a team can rally around. While it is true that Agile does not advocate leadership in terms of being the boss, Agile does espouse a concept of leadership in which leaders must become set the standard by which team members must perform.

Consequently, the actions and attitudes of the leader will make, or break, the entire team's performance. Hence, I would greatly encourage you, if you are in a leadership position, to take your role to heart and truly become a positive influence on your teammates.

Chapter 7: Useful Resources

So, at this point, I hope that I have managed to paint a clear picture of what Agile is, and how Scrum can become an effective methodology for you and your organization. Thus, this implies embracing the Agile mindset and making changes in your overall mentality to embrace the finer points of Scrum.

However, you might be asking yourself where you can begin. This is especially true if you are not familiar with Scrum or Agile. If this is the first time you have seriously dug into the Agile mindset, then you might be eager to learn more about how you can set down the path toward embracing Agile in order to harness its full potential.

While this book was certainly a great step in the right direction, you might be looking for additional resources which can help you get your journey in Agile off to a rocking start.

So, the first place to begin is this book. Please feel free to share the knowledge you have learned here with your colleagues and teammates. You can become an agent of change by implementing this knowledge in such a way that those around you can learn more about the Agile mindset and the finer points of Scrum.

You might also be interested in holding some training sessions or meetings in which you can discuss how Agile may benefit your organization and if Agile is truly right for you and your organization. While it is true that Agile has a cross-cutting application across various fields, there may be valid reasons why Agile might not be a good fit for your organization.

Nevertheless, I am sure that the more you learn about Agile, the more you will see how many of the underlying principles in Agile, and by extension Scrum, can be applied to your organization. Of course, this is not the type of process that can happen overnight, but it is worth taking a deeper look.

By giving Scrum some serious consideration, you will be opening the door to making some interesting changes in the way business is conducted in your organization. Of course, I have no doubt that your team is currently engaged in making the most of their opportunity to deliver value, they may not be fully aware of the potential that lies in embracing a framework, such as Scrum, which can bring a certain, "logic to the madness."

However, you might not feel entirely confident about leading a Scrum-oriented process. At least not yet. Hence, you might be looking for other sources in which you can gain further insights and perspectives on implementing Scrum in your organization.

Find a Great Agile Coach

One of the best sources of knowledge and experience in the Agile world is an experienced and reputable Agile Coach. A good Agile Coach will take you and your teammates through the rigors of Agile, more specifically Scrum, and help you see how implementing Scrum can help you improve your overall processes.

Also, an Agile Coach will work with you and your team in helping you improve your overall knowledge and understanding of Agile. In doing this, the Agile Coach will help all of the members involved in this transition process become keenly aware of how Agile can be put into practice in virtually all facets of your organization's operation. Therefore, you can rest assured that you will be able to make a strong case for the implementation of Agile within your organization.

In addition, a good Agile Coach is a type of person who can hold your hand through an entire Scrum project. They can sit on the sidelines while your team takes the field. When mistakes happen, the Agile Coach will be quick to help you find the proper solution to the shortcomings your team has made. This will enable your teammates to find their rightful place within the Agile mindset in such a way that you can take full advantage of their strengths while allowing them to grow out of any limitations they may have.

Of course, an Agile Coach may not come cheap, but the overall investment would certainly be worth the time and money. Nevertheless, your organization may not be in a position to take on a full-time consultant in this capacity.

So, what other options are out there for your team to become versed in Agile and Scrum?

The Multiplier Effect

One workaround that companies and organizations use when they don't have the means to bring in full-time consultants or expensive training companies is to have a handful of staff members get trained by the experts and then multiply their knowledge and expertise.

In doing this, the organization can ensure that growth as a result of the implementation of Agile and Scrum methodologies can be born from within the company. Considering that experts and consultants have the know-how to help your organization get off the ground, it's worth mentioning that there are equally qualified individuals within your organization who can also learn from the pros and then become excellent coaches in their own right.

So, your organization might choose to send some staff off to a training course, take a class at a local college, or take an online training course. These options open the discussion to some interesting possibilities.

First, does your staff really need to take time off work in order to attend a training seminar or a class?

If you believe that it is worth giving some staff members time off to attend in-person training, then you can certainly go down that path. However, you might find that taking time off from work may not be the wisest course of action. After all, the time that staff is not working means that it is time in which tasks are not getting done.

Now, you could ask the staff to go in their free time. This may, or may not, be appealing to some. But you can be sure that if someone takes a class in their free time, it is because they are committed to learning. But this brings us to another interesting possibility: online courses.

There are several companies which offer online training courses in Agile and Scrum. They offer a number of courses and certifications which you can pursue. While not all folks are interested in becoming officially certified, holding one such certification is a great way in which you can earn some valuable credentials. Consequently, some folks are keen on becoming certified in the fields of Agile and Scrum.

Here are some of the most renowned companies in the online Agile training business:

- **Scrumstudy.com.** They offer all sorts of courses and training programs ranging from free introductory courses to full-fledged certifications. I would encourage you to check out their free courses and then look into their paid options. I believe you will find some interesting options for yourself and your teammates.
- **Scrum.org**. This company is very similar to Scrumstudy. They offer a learning path which leads to certification in addition to providing some free content to learners. This company also provides classes and training seminars which you can book in-person depending on your location.
- **Scrum Alliance**. This is one of the largest players in the Agile training world. They have a series of courses and training seminars which you can attend both online and in person. So, I would encourage you to take a closer look at how the Scrum Alliance may be able to offer you the right training solution.

- **Project management Institute** (PMI). PMI is the company behind the traditional Project Management Professional (PMP) certification. This is the most widely-respected project management certification out there. Holders of the PMP certification are heralded as pros in their field. However, PMI was a bit slow in embracing the Agile movement. Nevertheless, PMI has its own Agile training program now which is certainly worth checking out. PMI has local chapters all over the world. So, it's certainly worth giving them a look.

- **Agile Alliance**. Just like the Scrum Alliance, the Agile Alliance is focused on the broader Agile movement. So, their focus is not just on Scrum, but on all things Agile. This is a great source of information which you can check out. They have a very extensive repository of information which can check out for free. So, I would highly recommend their website for your Agile research needs.

So, there you have it. I hope you are eager to get started on the road that leads to an Agile mindset. I am sure that the information you have found in this book will help you build a convincing argument for Scrum.

However, if after reading this book you are not convinced that Agile might be right for you, then that's alright, too. As I have mentioned earlier, Agile isn't for everyone, and it certainly isn't for every organization. Nevertheless, I hope that you will give Agile and Scrum a chance. After all, you have nothing to lose but everything to gain in a new, dynamic Agile world.

Conclusion

Thank you for taking the time to read this book. If you have made it this far, it is because you are truly interested in the topic and engaged in this discussion. By taking the time to learn more about Agile and Scrum, you are opening the door to bigger and better possibilities, not just for yourself, but for your organization as well.

If you have decided to read this book as an individual who is looking to improve their skills, then you have taken a big step toward becoming an Agile expert. The next step is to learn more about Agile and Scrum. By learning more, you can decide if pursuing a formal certification is right for you. I encourage you to continue reading part 2 for the other book in this series: *"Scrum Mastery. Agile leadership to take your team's performance from good to great."*

If you do choose to pursue a formal certification, the check out the companies which I have mentioned in the previous chapter. They have reputable training programs and can provide you with a proper path to become certified.

On the other hand, if you choose to not pursue certification, then that's great, too. I just hope that you can embrace the Agile mindset in everything you do at work and in your personal life, as well. As such, being Agile isn't just about getting stuff done at work; it's also perfectly applicable to your daily life. After all, you can search to provide your friends and family with value on a consistent basis.

If you are interested in pursuing further learning of Agile and Scrum at an institutional level, then, by all means, take the knowledge you have learned in this book and share it with your colleagues. You can hold meetings and even a training seminar in order to present your colleagues and teammates with a solid overview of what Agile is all about. Then, you can make a decision, as a team, to pursue Agile as part of your organization's philosophy.

In addition, your choice to embrace Agile as a project management methodology will certainly help provide guidance and direction to your teammates in such a way that you can ensure the success of your team in everything you do.

So, I would greatly encourage you to take the time to make the most of the opportunities you have to improve yourself and your organization's acumen by learning as much as you can about Agile. Bear in mind that Agile advocates for a continuous learning and improvement mentality. Therefore, this is a great way to live by those rules.

Finally, I would like to thank you once again for taking the time to read this book. I am well aware that there are other choices out there on this topic.

But, by reading this book, you have validated my hard work and experience.

As such, I would like to encourage you to leave a comment and be honest about what you thought of the information contained in this book. I am positive that others will find it very useful. So, if you have found this book to be interesting and informative, be sure to let others know about it!

Part 2:

Scrum Mastery

Agile Leadership to Take Your Team's Performance from Good to Great

Jeff Cohn

Part 2: Table of Contents

Introduction

Thank you for choosing, "*Scrum Mastery. Agile leadership to take your team's performance from good to great.*" If you are reading this, it is because you are serious about getting the most out of what Agile and Scrum have to offer you and your organization.

If you are new to the world of Agile, I would encourage you to check out the previous volume to this book entitled, "*Scrum Fundamentals. A beginner's guide to mastery of the Scrum project management methodology.*" In it, you will find a trove of information and knowledge regarding the worlds of Scrum and Agile.

Also, you will learn more about how Scrum and Agile can fit your organization so that you can run your projects, and your company as whole, under the "Agile mindset." This is a very useful approach as it will enable you to focus on delivering value to your customers while empowering your team to be at its best.

If you are experienced in the world of Agile and Scrum, then you have come to the right place. While there are other books available on this subject, you will be hard pressed to find a single tome that can deliver the amount of information and practical examples that you will find here.

Consequently, I would like to encourage you to take your time with this book. This isn't the type of book which you can just breeze through and be done with it. Since it is packed with information and actionable advice, you will surely find something new every time you go through it. I have taken great care in making sure that you have everything you need in order to get the most out of your use of Scrum and Agile in your organization.

So, when building upon the fundamentals of Agile and Scrum, many practitioners run into some dead ends. For instance, may Scrum practitioners are clear on the underlying philosophy regarding the methodology itself, but may be unclear as to the actual roles of the main players in Scrum. While the role of Scrum developers is generally straightforward, the role of the Scrum Master and the Product Owner tends to be a bit more complex to understand.

The reason for this is that traditional project management methodologies espouse a much more rigid and hierarchical structure in which the main focus of the leadership roles is to direct and coordinate activities. There is a clear pecking order which must be respected. Moreover, leadership roles in a traditional project management environment aim to establish clear roles for responsibility and competence.

Within the Agile mindset, responsibility is shared across the team. Therefore, one person is not "responsible" for the project. Rather, the entire team is responsible in such a way that they are tasked with pushing the project through to the end. In addition, the credit for the project's success is also evenly distributed among all of the members of the team. This not only breeds empowerment, but it also breeds a sense of satisfaction and success.

Another of the most important elements that will be discussed in this book is how to build a successful Scrum team. Often, practitioners don't have a clear perspective as how to a successful Scrum team can be built. As such, a lack of understanding in this regard may lead to complex situations that lead to failure.

Therefore, it is crucial that you, as a Scrum practitioner, have a clear understanding of the methodology and how that methodology relates to the overall mechanics of a successful Scrum team. So, we will drill down into the mechanics of a successful Scrum team insofar as determining best practices, based on experience, which can help you gain the right edge in the world of Agile project management.

As such, your understanding of Scrum and Agile will enable you to develop the right types of patterns and behaviors which will foster communication and an overall sense of accomplishment in your team. As your team gains more traction, they will develop a greater sense of empowerment. This will not only lead to a higher level of motivation, but also to a higher level of self-satisfaction. Thus, this creates a feedback loop which cannot be compared to anything else.

One other vital element that will be dealt with in this book is the scaling of Scrum. In the previous book, we touched on how Scrum is not just limited to one team, one Scrum Master and one Product Owner. Scrum can be scaled up as much as needed. That means that regardless of a project's scope and requirements, Scrum is able to address project objectives in such a way that project deliverables can be met on time and with the desired quality.

Naturally, large scope projects utilizing Scrum as its underlying project management methodology do require more careful planning and coordination, but that is true of any project under any methodology. Thus, it's vital that project leaders do their best to make sure that every project component is in its rightful spot.

So, as we are set to begin, it's important to keep an open mind. I know that this book will challenge your previous notions on project management, including what you may have already seen and read about Scrum and Agile. That is why our intent is to provide you with greater insight into what the latest Scrum and Agile practices have to offer project management professionals, or virtually any professional in the realm of business administration.

I am sure that the insights which you will find in this book will be useful both in your daily management practices, as well as, any project you would be looking to coordinate. Please bear in mind that there is no project too big, or too small, to have an appropriate measure of Scrum incorporated into it.

So, let's get started with this discussion. We have quite a bit to talk about. And, I am sure you are as eager as I am to get the ball rolling.

Chapter 1: What makes a great Scrum Master?

When you think of a Scrum Master, what comes to mind?

Is it:

     a.   An all-knowing sage who is a Scrum encyclopedia

     b.   The fearless leader who knows exactly what to do at all times

     c.   The project manager who is in charge of all operations

     d.   "The boss"

If you picked any of the above answers, you'd be wrong.

In the Agile world, leadership is not about being the boss, being right or having the power. Within the Agile domain, being in a leadership position means you are there to help your team win any way possible.

So, "win" is the operative word in this discussion.

Often, folks who come up through the ranks in the project management profession feel they are entitled to having control, power or any other type of dominance over the way the project is carried out. In fact, this is true of projects run under a traditional project management style in which the last thing that people are looking for in the team work, but rather, just getting the job done.

Conseq uently, being a leader in the Agile and Scrum world means that you need to check your ego at the door. If you are able to let your ego sit in the backseat, then you will have a great chance to lead your team in such a way that they will be successful.

So, what is all of this talk of Agile and Scrum?

If you are new to the world of Agile project management methodology, I would encourage you to drill down and really get a feel for the underlying philosophy that supports the entire Agile movement.

If you are a grizzled veteran of the Agile world, then I am sure you can come to appreciate the finer points of the underlying philosophy that holds up the entire Agile world.

Agile is all about getting things done as best as possible and as quickly as possible. It is really that simple. There are no gimmicks or tricks. The underlying philosophy that supports Scrum is good, old-fashioned team work and elbow grease.

There are no secret mantras that your team needs to chant before starting the day.

There are no special formulas to making things happen.

All there is, is a solid foundation which enables your team to work under clear guidelines and rules. So, you are essentially taking the guesswork out of your project management approach. What you are doing is enabling your people to make their own decisions based on their own sound judgment and understanding.

A brief history of Agile

Agile isn't exactly new, but it hasn't been around for too long, either. In fact, the concept of Agile was born out of the disgruntled nature of software developers that couldn't find a proper approach to apply to their software development projects.

The fact that developers were unhappy about traditional project management approaches led to a group of 11 software engineers come together to develop the Agile manifesto.

The Agile manifesto is the document with the underlying philosophy supporting the entire Agile movement. It is a conceptual framework which places the onus on the team working on the project management and not the almighty leader who has all the answers and bears the entire responsibility for the success, or failure, of the project.

The most important aspect of the Agile manifesto is the shift in mindset from a hierarchical structure, to a flat one in which the customer takes center stage while the team is left to organize itself in a collaborative manner.

As such, here is the actual text of the Agile manifesto as conceived by its creators:

We are uncovering better ways of developing software by doing it and helping others do it. Through this work we have come to value:

Individuals and interactions over processes and tools

Working software over comprehensive documentation

Customer collaboration over contract negotiation

Responding to change over following a plan

That is, while there is value in the items on the right, we value the items on the left more.

As you can see from the Agile manifesto itself, the focus is on delivering value at all times. Value is what drives the production of software in such a way that it consistently delivers value to customers at all stages of the project.

Notice how the Agile manifesto makes a point of highlighting "individuals and interactions" and not processes. Also, it values working software over documentation while encouraging collaboration over contracts. Finally, responding to change is the key element as compared to following a plan.

Definitely, Agile espouses as a methodology which is flexible and dynamic so that project teams are consistently focused on embracing change rather than sticking to a rigid plan at all costs. As such, change is the number one item on the minds of all Agile project managers.

Now, one of the mot common objections to Agile methodologies is that it has been specifically designed for the software industry. And while it is true that it was born out of the software industry, it has since grown to a much more cross-cutting appeal in which it can be applied in several industries and not just software development.

Later on in this book, we will get a chance to dig deeper into how Scrum and Agile can be implemented in virtually any type of industry and not just software or IT. Most importantly, the Agile mindset is a fundamental shift in the overall perception a company has of its methods and means of running the business.

That being said, it's important to focus on the fact that Agile is not about implementing a technology that will solve all of the challenges that project managers face on a regular basis. While it does create a discipline within project management as a whole, Agile is not about developing the perfect system; it's about creating an environment which is conducive to success.

Three pillars of Scrum

Given the fact that Agile, and consequently Scrum, are all about empowering project team members and providing value to customers, it is only fitting that the three pillars of Scrum are based on three core principles centered around people:

1. Transparency
2. Inspection
3. Adaptation

These principles are rooted in enabling individuals to take control over their tasks and responsibilities in such a way that there is a maximization of output through collaborative endeavors.

As such, each of the pillars that make up Scrum project management methodology are a direct spin off Agile. Thus, it is important to note that Agile is the overarching framework which Scrum is based on. These pillars are a direct representation of how Agile is conceived and how Scrum can be implemented to suit the needs of individual projects.

Transparency

The first pillar is transparency.

And, needless to say, this one is a biggie.

Transparency is one of the most important factors that plays into effective Scrum implementation and accountability is an especially big deal.

Now, traditional project management methodologies espouse having a project manager who bears the ultimate responsibility of a project's success. If the project bears the results it was intended to, then the project manager is a hit. If the project fails, the project manager is the one to blame.

This approach creates a single point of accountability which virtually zaps any potential for growth and innovation on the part of individual team members. In fact, under a traditional approach, individual members are seen as interchangeable pieces which can be replaced as needed.

Indeed, this is a clear reflection on management philosophies and practices which are not conducive to a collaborative environment. By the same token, the project manager needs to supervise and make sure that everyone does everything they are supposed to be doing. This not only drains time and attention away from actual work, but it can also lead to attrition both on the part of the team members and project manager.

This is where Scrum offers a fantastic alternative. Scrum draws from the Agile manifesto and places greater importance on people rather than processes. This entails that understanding what each team member brings to the table becomes a vital component of determining the broader approach the Scrum team can utilize in a project.

When a collaborative, self-organizing approach is encouraged, team members are much more motivated and willing to find the best way to get the job done. Often, this leads to innovation and alternate solutions to complex problems.

Collaborative teams allow everyone to pitch in on equal terms while allowing the sum of the forces to multiply their efforts. Of course, being self-organizing also implies being that each team member needs to be accountable for their actions and their role on the team.

This is where transparency becomes such a key issue. Here, transparency pertains to individual team members within the team's dynamic, but it also refers to transparency with the customer. Since Scrum continuously produces "working software", the customer can see the direction the final product is taking at various stages of the project. This is where customers have the opportunity to see if the path the final product is taking truly meets their expectations.

Inspection

The second pillar refers to inspection. However, inspection does not refer to the traditional manufacturing type of inspection in which outputs are carefully scrutinized in order to determine where potential defects may lie.

Sure, Scrum advocates close review of outputs in order to ensure that they comply with customer specifications, but the fact of the matter is that inspection is part of a broader process of continuous improvement. What that means is that Scrum teams are always in search of improving processes and outputs. Therefore, it is crucial to have a clear understanding of what issues may arise with the actual implementation of the final solution.

Scrum also enables all members of the team to keep track of the entire team's work. This implies that each member has the opportunity to see what everyone else is doing at any given point in time.

Does this mean that anyone can inspect the work being done?

Yes, however, the point is not to be overly critical of the work being done. Rather, this affords everyone the opportunity to see how their work fits within the grander scheme of things. Based on that, individual members may be able to pick up on something which may have been overlooked by the rest of the team.

It is also important to understand that individual team members must be open-minded in the sense that feedback is intended to improve and not to criticize for the sake of criticism. The feedback that comes from both the team itself and the customer is intended to address the potential issues that may arise throughout project development. This allows for a proactive approach focused on developing trust and confidence among all project stakeholders.

Adaptation

The third pillar refers to dealing with change.

In any project context, change is one of the most common issues that project teams must face.

Change is inevitable. There is nothing that can be done to stop change. Change will happen as naturally as night and day. The issue then becomes how to deal with such change.

Traditionally, one of the aims of project management is to reduce the amount of uncertainty and change in projects in order to make them as predictable as possible. The reasoning behind this attitude is that project managers face constant pressure with regard to sticking to schedules and budget. There is nothing worse in the project management world than to have a project run over schedule and over budget. This not only speaks negatively on the project manager and team, but it also implies that the project wasn't planned properly.

Nevertheless, it is not always a question of planning and lack of management skills that may cause a project to go haywire. In fact, there are n number of possibilities which would cause a project to go off the rails. As such, the issue does not lie with individual problems. Rather, it lies with the way these individual issues are dealt with.

Detractors and critics of Scrum often point to the reactionary nature of adapting to change. And yes, that is true: a great deal of what Scrum advocates is reacting to change as it happens, or as it is requested. But the truth of the matter is that adaptability in Agile and Scrum lies at the very core of its conceptual framework.

Often, experienced Scrum teams will be able to anticipate issues and thereby implement change solutions before the potential issue actually becomes an issue. This is one of the most important virtues that change management has under the Scrum umbrella.

At the end of the day, Scrum Masters are encouraged to aid their team in identifying potential risks so that issues may be addressed early on in the sprint rather than at any other point in the process.

Being a great Scrum Master

So, this brings us back to the original point in this chapter: what makes a great Scrum Master?

In short, a great Scrum Master is only as good as their team.

This implies that leadership in Agile is not about being superior, but rather, it is about serving others. I know that may seem a bit counterintuitive with the traditional concept of leadership. In fact, most management programs call for leaders to be the fearless guide that has all the answers.

Even in more progressive management training programs, leaders in the Agile domain are considered to be superior in all aspects to their team members. This is a requisite trait that is needed in order to "earn" the respect of peers.

The truth of the matter is that the term "Scrum Master" refers to the level of mastery an individual has in Scrum methodology, but not in terms of being a "master" of some domain. In fact, Scrum Masters have a dual role.

First, Scrum Masters are expected to provide guidance and leadership to their team while allowing their team to find the best way to implement the methodology as prescribed by best practices.

Second, Scrum Masters are known as "subservient leaders." What this means is that a

Scrum Master should not be bossing everyone around making sure things get done. On the contrary, the role of the Scrum Master is to ensure that their team has everything they need in order to get the job done.

This sounds more like a coordination role. In fact, it is. A Scrum Master is a coordinator who is in charge of making sure that everything is being done the way it is supposed to be done.

But, wait a minute, that sounds like a boss.

Not in the traditional sense.

A good Scrum Master is able to "direct traffic" in such a way that all of the players on the team know where they are going and how to get there. Since teams are self-organizing, the Scrum Master is basically on the sidelines acting like a coach.

This implies that when the Scrum Master detects something that is not going according to plan, they have the prerogative of bringing it up at meetings. This is part of the Scrum feedback loop that is intended at developing appropriate mechanisms and procedures.

The three platinum principles

Therefore, leadership in Agile and Scrum is based on the three platinum principles.

These principles, much like the three pillars, are intended to provide a road map for all team members to follow. While it is true that there may be more than one way to achieve similar results, the fact of the matter is that it is vital for all team members to go in the same direction. This will ensure that efforts are concentrated on where they matter most. Most importantly, the direction the team takes will be determined by the team itself. As such, the road travelled should be one with which each team member is comfortable.

Consequently, the three principles are listed as follows:

1. Resisting formality
2. Thinking and acting as a team
3. Visualizing rather than writing

On the surface, these principles might seem rather counterintuitive. They don't necessarily adhere to what is considered "normal" in the business world. Thus, we need to take a closer look at each one of these principles.

Resisting formality

This first principle really stands out.

What does it mean to "resist formality"?

It might sound like the team will walk around in their pajamas all day playing video games while they work.

Formality, in an Agile sense, is about a rigid

structure which cannot be modified for anything in the world. As such, Agile frowns upon having set structures which do not foster creativity and embrace change. Thus, formality is seen as valuing processes over people. Consequently, the spirit of Agile is not being fully embraced.

Being Agile is all about breaking down barriers and finding solutions to problems and challenges which may have posed a considerable risk in the past. For instance, the phrase, "it's always been that way" is a huge no-no in the Agile mindset.

Therefore, Scrum teams are encouraged to push the envelope and test traditional assumptions. If something has always been done in a certain way, then perhaps it's time to try something new. After all, innovation leads to breakthroughs which can significantly alter the course of things.

As for the Scrum Master, "formality" refers to the being the "almighty" leader who is always right. In fact, the true role of the Scrum Master challenges all assumptions of what leadership should be in the business world. As a matter of fact, leadership under this context is exerted by exhibiting the traits that make a team successful rather than just issuing orders.

Thinking and acting as team

The second principle harkens back to the collaborative nature of Scrum.

The name "Scrum" was conceived from Rugby. In this sport, all of the players on the field act a whole since the action never stops. Once the ball is put into play, the two teams battle for control of the ball. Once one team has control, they must all work together in order protect each other from their opponents and eventually reach the other end of the field.

This is exactly what Scrum is all about.

The fact that the Scrum methodology calls for teamwork, that implies that any one team member may have the ball at any time, but must also be ready to pass it off to the next player. Once a team member has passed off the ball, then their role is to protect the player with the ball. In this type of approach, there is no waiting on one side of the field in order to "get open."

In this approach, you must be both open and ready to protect your teammates at all times.

Hence, Agile leaders are all about fostering teamwork. Teamwork is seen as the core attitude which will make projects successful. If teamwork cannot be encouraged, then it is safe to say that the project will be met with considerable headwinds.

Does this mean that a lack of teamwork will doom a project?

Not necessarily.

What it does mean is that adequate teamwork will make everyone's lives a lot easier. That is why the Scrum Master should focus on building a close-knit team. This can be achieved through a number of actions. But regardless of how it is achieved, it is up to the Scrum Master to make sure that any potential issues among team members are to be dealt with immediately. The last thing a Scrum Master wants is to have personal differences get in the way of the collaborative nature of the project.

Visualizing rather writing

The third platinum principle ties in with the Agile concept of "working software over comprehensive documentation."

Sure, all projects need to have certain details in black and white. In fact, it would be irresponsible to commit things to memory while leaving agreements and accords as simple words.

However, this does not mean that teams should focus their efforts on producing manuals, handbooks, and reports. Scrum teams are successful at visualizing what the best solution is and how any potential solution can lead to improving the quality of the output. Thus, Scrum Masters are also tasked with helping the project team visualize what the best solution for the team would be. That is, what the best way of doing something would be.

This is a solution that only the team can develop. The Scrum Master needs to resist the temptation of imposing their will on the team. Naturally, the Scrum Master has valuable input as to what the team may or may not be able to do. But ultimately, the way things are done is a collaborative team decision.

This implies that leadership within Agile must look toward building a consensus on the approach that a project will take on while ensuring that team members have everything they need in order to make that vision happen.

Bringing it all together

At this point, I am confident that you have a good understanding of how Scrum and Agile conceive project management. Nevertheless, it is also important to bring everything together in a practical example.

I recall an experience I had some time ago.

There was a very bright young lady who was at the helm of a project which utilized Scrum. This young lady was in charge of bringing the team together and setting them up for success. She was totally committed to building her team on Agile principles.

Once the team was assembled, she asked everyone to "check their egos at the door" (she actually said that). She made the point that everyone was equally good. This wasn't a team with one good player and a supporting cast. This was a team of stars.

She was also clear that her role was to facilitate and coordinate the actions among all team members. Her job was to make sure that everyone understood what the project was about, and how each, individual member could use their talents in achieving the project outcomes.

After the work breakdown was determined, team members distributed tasks among themselves based on who was better suited for each task. The team quickly divided the work up amongst themselves and got to work.

The Scrum Master stood in the background monitoring progress and making sure that everyone stayed on track. She would have regular one-on-one chats with all members in addition to the regular daily meeting.

These one-on-one sessions were not about sitting down and having a formal review. These were just informal chats about how things were going and if there were any issues that each developer faced. More often than not, questions would arise about methodology, how to do something, and the best way to do it.

Whenever a team member did not know how to do something, or perhaps wasn't sure about the best way to do it, the Scrum Master would pose the question to the team. Sure enough, someone knew the answer.

While the execution of this project was not perfect, the attitude of the Scrum Master had been. She was clear that her role was to support her team at all times while ensuring that everyone felt valued and appreciated.

In the end, the project hit all its targets on time. The customer was thrilled with the results. It was a successful project that owed its success to the positive attitude of all team members and the selfless nature of its project lead, the Scrum Master.

Chapter 2: Anti-patterns in Scrum and Agile

In the first chapter of this book, we took an in-depth look at what leadership in Agile is and the specific role a Scrum Master plays within a Scrum project.

We also understood the collaborative nature of Agile in such a way that Scrum teams are driven by teamwork and not individual success. Often, individuals lose sight of the fact that individual performance is augmented by team success rather than the other way around.

Sure, there are sports, industries, companies, endeavors, and so on, which are driven by one individual. Think of a great sports star such as Michael Jordan.

Michael Jordan was the centerpiece of the Chicago Bulls NBA dynasty in the 1990s. However, Michael Jordan could never have won all of those championships without the help of his teammates. The likes of Scottie Pippen, Dennis Rodman and Steve Kerr, to name a few, were instrumental in helping the Bulls to six championships during Michael Jordan's career.

Does that mean that the aforementioned players were a supporting cast of characters which helped him reach success? Actually, they were equal. Except they played different positions. Moreover, when Jordan wasn't having a good game, was hurt, or was under intense pressure from the other team, it was his teammates who picked up the slack and led the team.

This a great example of what Scrum is all about. The Scrum team members are individuals who are good, if not the best, at what they do. They are adept at making things happen and getting the job done. They are able to work together and come up with the best possible solution to their customer's requests.

However, nothing good comes without its caveats.

In Scrum, as with any other project management methodology, there is always the risk of things not going right. It might be something simple which can be addressed immediately. But if left unattended, it may fester and grow into a larger issue.

Or, the project may be facing considerable headwinds and the project team needs to rally together in order to get the job done. When such circumstances occur, teamwork becomes paramount in overcoming such headwinds.

The Scrum Master, more than ever, acts like the Bulls' legendary coach Phil Jackson, standing on the sidelines making sure the team is working well together and picking up on things that perhaps the team itself may not be aware of.

This collaborative attitude ensures that team members stay focused and in sync with everything happening around them. As such, the Scrum Master is hardly the star. They are just ensuring that the coordination done among the team works perfectly.

Nevertheless, there are several pitfalls that Scrum practitioners need to pay attention to. These are called "anti-patterns" as they go against the prescribed Agile methodology. So, in this chapter, we will take a closer look at how these anti-patterns may develop, and how they may end up dragging the team down and holding back optimal results.

Not updating progress

The first of the anti-patterns in this chapter pertains to not tracking and updating progress.

I have decided to tackle this topic first as there is much to talk about.

Tracking progress is one of the essential functions in any project management methodology. Progress, in simple terms, can be tracked by the number of tasks completed.

Also, a broader measure of success can be seen in the number of objectives, or in the case of Scrum, user stories, completed.

Tracking progress has both an administrative and psychological function.

Firstly, it is an administrative function since tracking progress allows the team to see what has already been achieved and what is left to do. This is the right way in order to determine how far along the project is and if the remaining tasks will be met within the time frame that was established at the outset of the project or individual sprint.

When the team is clear on the progress that is being made, all team members can feel confident in the work they are doing. Motivation is increased, as there is a greater sense of satisfaction in the work being done.

Secondly, it is also a psychological factor since it allows the team to see the finish line getting closer.

Think of it this way: you are a sailor on a ship that has been at high seas for a long time. You may feel discouraged and even desperate at the thought of there being nothing else around you except water. This can lead to a sailor flipping out and becoming mad. Believe me, sailors went through this back in the day.

Now, imagine for a second that you see land. After all that time at sea, you finally get a glimpse of land. Sure, land may still be very far away, but you have your first sight of the finish line.

So, tracking progress is much the same way. Of course, I don't intend to make a Scrum sprint seem like being at sea for countless days. The point that I want to drive home is the fact that tracking progress allows team members to find their bearings and become confident in the fact that their work is counting for something.

Under Scrum methodology, it is the Scrum Master's job to make sure that progress is being tracked accordingly. Sure, it's up to the entire team to make sure that there is a proper track of everything that is being completed throughout the project, but the ultimate responsibility of tracking progress is up to the Scrum Master.

As such, Scrum utilizes the "board" to track progress.

A Scrum board is a visual device which measures the progress of the tasks being completed This board intends to provide a visual representation of the tasks being completed and the ones which are still in progress.

So, the issue does not lie in the failure to update the board as such, but rather, in the failure to track progress. Of course, you might think that it doesn't matter if the board is not update because everyone is on the same page on what they are doing.

Well, you might be wrong. In fact, not tracking progress can lead to a team falling behind since they don't know where they clearly stand. Also, the team may lose focus on what they are truly meant to do. Thus, failure to track progress will lead to teams duplicating tasks or missing tasks altogether simply because they don't have the input they need in order to follow up on their progress.

Finally, the failure to track progress speaks on how the leadership in the project is committed to the overall project. In essence, it means there is a high degree of disregard for the project itself and the level of commitment that the leaders, in this case the Scrum Master, have for their role in the project.

So, the Scrum Master needs to be fully committed to seeing the project come to fruition. By being fully committed, the Scrum Master will be sure to follow through on their tasks in addition to encouraging their team to follow through on theirs. This breeds excellence in the way tasks are conducted throughout the lifecycle of the project.

Taking on work outside of the sprint

Each sprint should be a carefully planned exercise.

At the outset of each sprint, the Sprint Planning Meeting serves as the means by which the Scrum Master and the Development Team (this meeting may also include the participation of the Product Owner) define the scope of the sprint in order to determine the amount of tasks that will be completed, in addition to defining which tasks will be completed and which ones may be left over for ensuing sprints.

Now, during the Sprint Planning Meeting, prioritization should be given to requisite tasks, that is, tasks that need to be completed in order for future tasks to build on. This implies that requisite tasks get a higher prioritization as compared to other tasks which may contribute to the completion of a user story but may not necessarily be completed in that particular sprint.

When work is carefully delineated, the Scrum team is focused and engaged on what needs to be done. The Scrum team keeps track of the work completed and the work remaining to be done. This provides a discipline for the work that is to be done throughout the sprint.

However, what happens when change comes into the picture?

If there is a request for change on the part of the customer or even the Product Owner, the Development Team must find a way to incorporate those changes into future sprints especially since the current sprint cycle has work that has already been planned and assigned.

But what is the big deal with taking on work that was not originally planned in the sprint?

You see, the problem is not taking on additional work as such. The problem is the additional work means that time, attention and resources will be deviated from the originally planned tasks into new tasks which may not necessarily contribute to the objectives of that specific sprint.

In fact, there are cases where the user stories and tasks planned at the beginning of the sprint were not the right ones. That may even lead to the cancellation of a sprint (more on that later on). The fact remains that doing something "extra" may hinder your team's chances of getting valuable work done.

Consider this: the client has requested additional features or functionalities which weren't part of the original plan. So, the Product Owner sits down with the client and makes them see that this implies additional work not contemplated during the project planning phase. The client agrees with this and also agrees to pay extra for the additional work requested.

What do you do in this case?

First, the wrong answers.

You decide to see in which sprints you can fit the additional work requested and ask your team to incorporate it into their planning. After all, you need to meet the project's deadline as agreed upon at the beginning of the project itself.

While this solution may seem logical on the surface, you would be overloading your team. What happens is that you have already planned the number of sprints it would take to achieve the project outcomes. So, if you decide to take on more work within the same time frame, then you would be over extending your team.

By doing this, you may end up missing deadlines and thereby your targets. You may incur in cost and time overruns. Ultimately, you could jeopardize the entire project's integrity. So, you would need to carefully plan incorporating new tasks into the sprints you have already designed.

Also, you could hire more team members. On the whole this may actually work. You might be able to pull it off if you are able to find someone who can complete the new tasks during the actual time your project is underway.

Now, there is something to be said about bringing new team members in mid-project or mid-sprint. If you find yourself needing to add more team members or having to replace members, it's best to do this at the beginning of a new sprint and not mid-way. Sure, there might be extenuating circumstances in which you have to do this. For example, you might lose a team member due to a sudden illness and there is no reasonable way the other team members can pick up the slack.

In fact, there may be such circumstances in which you may end up having to cancel the sprint altogether as the team may lose a significant amount of members. This is hardly the ideal case, but you would certainly have to consider it rather than drag on a sprint that would lead to poor results.

The right answer in this case would be to add a sprint, or multiple sprints, in order to accommodate for the new requirements. If the customer is aware of the fact that they are requesting changes which were not a part of the original planning, then the customer should also agree to having additional sprints created in order to account for the additional work that will be done.

This is an important aspect that needs to be taken into account since additional features and functionalities means additional work. It is really that simple. So, it pays to be clear on what change requests imply to you and your Development Team.

No "work in progress" limit

A work in progress is just that, a work in progress.

However, when does a work in progress become a target which was not achieved?

This is a fair question to consider. After all, there is a logical point in which a task that was not completed becomes a task that was failed to be achieved.

This implies the need to set a boundary at which the "work in progress" becomes a "work not done."

There are a couple of ways of approaching this.

Firstly, the "work in progress" designation applies only to those tasks which were not completed during the sprint. If a task is yet to be completed at the end of a sprint, then it should be deemed a "work not done." This designation means that the team failed to achieve this objective.

So, at the Sprint Retrospective Meeting, the Scrum Master and the Development Team (with the participation of the Product Owner), can go over the reasons why the task was not achieved and how this could have been avoided.

Of course, the number of reasons why a task is not completed can be numerous. But the fact of the matter is that the Development Team needs to have a firm understanding of where things went wrong, and why it is necessary to understand this for the sake of future sprints.

Furthermore, the Scrum team can now decide if the task will be included in an upcoming sprint or dropped altogether. This is important to consider as the team may have decided to include a task which was not needed or perhaps planned too much work.

If the team took on too much work at the outset of the sprint, then the team may choose to revise the ways in which it decides what tasks to include and the amount of time needed to complete them. If the task was unnecessary, then the team must understand why it was included in order to avoid including needless tasks in the future.

Since Scrum is all about getting work done efficiently, then including work that is not needed may result in highly inefficient project management. As such, it's a rather clear reason why Scrum teams should not take on any work that wasn't originally intended in a sprint.

Of course, there is nothing wrong with admitting that a task was not completed and therefore needing to determine where and when it must be completed. The main point here is knowing and understanding that there is a point when the task is an official "failure."

So, it is up to the Scrum Master and even the Product Owner to sit down during the Sprint Retrospective Meeting and go over the reasons why the sprint failed to deliver such results. Ultimately, being able to understand and determine where the problem took place will create a very good discipline for the team moving forward.

One other important note about work in progress limits. Often, project teams have the initiative to add on features and functionalities which the customer did not request, but that they feel would be beneficial to the project.

Now, it's one thing to correct a potential problem and it's another to do something you feel the customer will like. This approach is just asking for trouble. If you are adding features which the customer did not request, that will only lead to extra work being done, which was not contemplated at the beginning of the sprint, but that end up altering the scope of the project.

Sure, you might think that if you have some time left over you can get around to it. Well, it is not about filling up left over time. If you have more time left over at the end of the sprint, you can always use that time to test the product and make sure that everything is working the way it is supposed to. If you detect any bugs, you can take that time to work them out and correct any issues beforehand.

Bear in mind that by being focused and sticking to what you committed to, you will please your customer by delivering on your word and making sure that you have exactly what they need, when they need it. That is efficiency.

At the end of the day, the Product Owner needs to manage change in order to ensure that any change requests, either don't fall outside of the scope of the project or delay the final delivery of the product.

For instance, the customer decides that they don't like the layout and color schemes of a software application. So, they request changes to the layout. This may result in delaying the final delivery of the application by a certain amount of time. At that point, the customer needs to be aware that that change will delay the product's completion.

Also, if a customer realizes they want something else added to the product which they suddenly thought it needed, the Product Owner can negotiate to have it tacked on to the end of the sprint cycle. This will avoid overburdening the project team with unnecessary tasks that will lead them to missing deadlines and racking up uncompleted tasks.

So, it certainly pays to be clear with the customer about what change requests mean and how they can impact the overall completion of the project.

Not cancelling a bad sprint

This one is a biggie.

We have talked about cancelling a sprint throughout this chapter. But, can you really cancel a sprint?

Of course!

However, it should be noted that we are not talking about cancelling a sprint just because something went wrong. Cancelling a sprint should be seen as a last resort type of situation.

So, under which circumstances should a sprint be cancelled?

Let's consider some practical situations.

Firstly, you have a Development Team consisting of 6 members. The team is underway with a sprint when suddenly one team member has fallen ill. They are sick and cannot come into work for at least a couple of weeks. Given that you have a four-week sprint, that's basically half the sprint. So, your team decides to suck it up and divide the tasks among the remaining five members.

At this point, you feel that you may have to work some overtime, but you can get the job done. The rest of the team is willing to pick up the slack and get the job done. So, you keep moving. But what happens if you lose another team member for whatever reason?

All of a sudden you are now down to four members doing the work of six. In this case, you might want to consider shutting things down and reassessing the situation. After all, you hire more team members, but doing that mid-sprint may not work. It's not easy for someone to come in mid-sprint and just hit the ground running.

Also, you might find it hard to find a qualified individual to fill the voids left by the departing members. Based on that logic, the sprint would be over, and you might not have a sound replacement. Thus, given the circumstances, it might be best to shut everything down, get new team members on board, plan the new sprint and then take it from there.

Most Scrum Masters and Product Owners try to have "backups" for team members, that is, find folks who are willing to come on to the team on short notice. While this may not always be possible, it is always good to have folks in mind who can step in a pinch hit when needed.

Another situation which may lead to the cancellation of a sprint is inadequate planning. This can lead to a poor assessment of the work that needs to be done during the Sprint Planning Meeting. For example, the Scrum team sits down to go over everything that needs to be done. The work breakdown structure is done, and the sprint gets off and running. At some point it is determined that the team will not get all the work done by the end of the sprint.

Hence, a decision needs to be made: do you begin to cut out tasks and just do what you can, or do you stop the show and go back to the drawing board?

Considering the first option, you could potentially cut out tasks as long as they don't interfere with the development of the user stories for that sprint. However, care needs to be taken in order to ensure that the cutting out tasks does not lead to an overall ineffective sprint.

The second option, and perhaps the best one, would be to just shut everything down, and go back to the drawing board. In doing this, you are ensuring that the mistakes made in planning can be corrected so that the team knows where they stand.

The problem with this solution is that it may lead to the team falling behind in schedule. Of course, this is a big deal since falling behind implies either trying to make up the work later on or having to extend the duration of the project. Either way, it's not an ideal situation.

So, what to do then?

Often, it's best to be honest and talk with the customer. Since Agile advocates for transparency, the Scrum Master can let the Product Owner know what happened and thereby have a talk with the customer about how the problems can be solved.

Many times, it is possible to make up and get the ship back on track. But it's always best to be honest and make sure that there is always a transparent solution to everything that is being done. Bear in mind that Agile is rooted in trust and communication. So, communication is vital in ensuring that everything which is done, is done in such a way that all stakeholders are on the same page.

Final thoughts

When looking at the pitfalls which may befall a Scrum team, it's important to note that these caveats can be overcome by careful planning and consideration of the circumstances which surround the project team.

At the end of the day, "team" is the operative word. When the Scrum team actually works as a team, you are able to foster positive communication and ensure that everything which is done, is done is such a way that you are being transparent and honest with all of the stakeholders in the project. You can then be transparent about setbacks and correct them.

The worst thing that you could try to do is cover up what has happened and attempt to make up for lost time later on. Sure, this might be possible when circumstances aren't as complex. Nevertheless, it is always important to keep track within the team since keeping careful track will allow everyone to be on the same page.

As such, the most important thing to keep in mind is that being focused on what needs to be done will help you maintain the discipline you need in order to guarantee your project's success. By doing exactly what needs to be done, no more and no less, you can be sure that you will meet your targets on time and with the quality your team needs to deliver. Ultimately, you want to be seen as reliable and able to deliver on the promises you make. This is what Agile and Scrum are all about.

Chapter 3: Establishing effective team mechanics

In the previous chapter, we took a close look at the pitfalls which may befall a Scrum team as a part of the development of a project. Nevertheless, it is also important to consider what can be done in order to create an effective team. As such, having adequate planning and clear guidelines is just as important as developing the proper team mechanics.

Often, Scrum practitioners are not entirely clear on how a Scrum team should actually be run. Bear in mind that Scrum teams don't run quite the same as a regular project team would. Under a traditional project management approach, the team leader or project manager would assign tasks to be done. In addition, this project lead would be in charge of supervising everyone on the team and ensure that everything gets done accordingly.

Since Agile and Scrum advocate for a flat organizational structure, it's vital that the proper team mechanics be developed in order to ensure that the team is able to work on its own and develop the discipline which is needed to get the job done with minimal supervision.

At the end of the day, that is the key, underlying factor: being able to get the job done with minimal supervision.

So, in this chapter, we will be taking a closer look at how you can develop proper team mechanics in such a way that your project will run as smoothly as possible without having to resort to micromanaging in order to get the job done.

Let's take an in-depth look at the team mechanics which will ensure your team's overall success.

Good team member traits

This is one of the most important aspects to consider when building your team.

But, what do "good team member traits" mean?

That is a fair question.

Good team member traits imply having the necessary traits that will allow team members to be effective Scrum practitioners. This implies being committed to the supporting philosophy that is espoused in Scrum.

If a team member is not fully committed to the Agile mindset, then that opens the door for team members to end up developing attitudes which are detrimental to the overall team dynamic.

For instance, if a team member wants to dominate and become the team leader. Sure, there are people with naturally dominant personalities while there are others who are much more comfortable playing a passive role within the team.

Does this mean that team members who exhibit natural leadership qualities are welcome to take over while those who are less inclined to take the lead should sit back and just do what they are told?

Hardly.

Agile advocates for team members to get equal say and participation in the development of a project. So, this implies that team members who tend to dominate should be aware that their leadership skills can be put to good use by helping those who aren't as extroverted to contribute equally.

Also, it is up to the Scrum Master to manage personalities in order to avoid having one team member boss everyone around. Solving this issue may be as simple as just reminding everyone how important it is to work collaboratively during the

Daily Stand up Meeting. Other times, it may be so bad that team members may have to be replaced in order to end power struggles.

Since neither the Scrum Master nor the Product Owner are the "boss" of the project, team members must find the best way to work among themselves without having the influence of a boss telling them what to do.

That is why having qualities such as commitment and a collaborative attitude allow for successful Scrum teams. This is in addition to any technical skills which may be required in order to do the job that needs to be done as part of the project.

Here are some other qualities that Scrum team members should exhibit:

- Detail oriented
- Committed to excellence
- Strive for development
- Open-minded
- Proactive
- Service oriented

As you can see, these are mainly soft skills that Scrum team members need to exhibit throughout the course of a project in order to ensure that the work being done is actually successful. Of course, the requisite hard skills truly depend on the nature and scope of a project. As such, a software project requires a certain skill set whereas building a house requires a completely different skill set. At the end of the day, it's up to the Product Owner to understand what skills and traits are needed in order to meet the technical requirements of the project.

Self-organizing teams

Perhaps the most important team mechanic in Scrum is self-organizing teams.

This is a crucial factor that plays into Scrum. Since Scrum espouses a flat organizational structure, there is no need for an overbearing "boss" or "supervisor" who can come in and dictate what needs to be done. Sure, there are leadership roles, such as the Scrum Master, but at the end of the day, the Scrum Master does not dictate what is to be done. The decision of what should be done, and when it should be done, falls on the team as a whole.

So, during the Sprint Planning Meeting, the entire team needs to sit down and decide what will be done in that sprint, who will do what, and how it will be done. Based on that assessment, the team can get to work on the goals set forth.

In addition, it's important for the team to keep in mind that they are in charge of themselves. Therefore, this implies a greater role for personal accountability. So, if someone makes a mistake, they need to own up to it; it's not about assigning blame, but rather, it's about finding the right way to correct the mistake.

In addition, a self-organizing team must be honest about their limitations. They must be mature enough to understand when they can't do something, but also be honest about how much work can be reasonably done within the timeframe provided. What that means is that project teams should not purposely drag their feet just to make life easier for them. Bear in mind that the overarching plan is to make sure that the work that is done, is done within that reasonable time frame.

As such, allowing a team to run itself is all about empowering the team to take control and become proactive in the way they run the project. Since each sprint is planned by the Scrum team as whole, there is enough room to enable teams to base their decisions on their capabilities and limitations.

Ultimately, a self-organizing team is the epitome of collaborative work. Since everyone on the team has equal say in what is done and not done, the team is them able to make a realistic assessment of what each sprint would produce.

It is also important to keep in mind that the project team needs to have a broad idea of how long the actual project would take in order to budget the time needed in terms of the number of sprints which will be conducted. Naturally, the greater the number of sprints, the lesser the amount of work which needs to be done in each one. Ultimately, sprints can be divided in such a way that latter sprints can be used for alpha and beta testing.

These are decisions which the project team must make collectively in order to arrive at a reasonable assessment of what can and can't be done.

Transparent communication

One of the core tenets of Scrum and Agile is transparency.

Transparency is essential in enabling a clear path for the project team to carry out work in a sustainable pace while keeping project stakeholders up to speed on the project's progress. This is why keeping track of the project's progress is essential.

Transparency is also vital in determining how communication actually takes place within the group. Agile and Scrum foster an environment of trust in such a way that individuals are encouraged to be open about all aspects pertaining to the work to be done.

For instance, if a team member is having difficulty in conducting a specific task, they should be encouraged to ask for help. Often, it may boil down to the Scrum Master offering support on a technical level, or perhaps the team is lacking a specific tool which is needed in order to get the job done.

The project team may run out of a given material or may end up needing a tool they hadn't contemplated. When this happens, the team needs to be forthcoming so that the Scrum Master can find the way to provide them with the tool, or even information, that the project team needs.

Also, transparent communication happens between the project team and the customer. Both the project team and the customer need to be on the same page regarding the work that is being done and the progress being made. So, transparency in communication is intended to discourage the customer from springing up additional requests without considering the project team's capabilities.

In addition, the project team needs to be forthcoming with the customer if they happen to encounter a difficulty which may delay the final release of the project's outputs. If this should be the case, the project team needs to be clear about how the situation can be remedied and how they can deliver, within a reasonable time frame, on the final release of the project.

Then, there's the topic of cost. If the project should overrun in cost, for whatever reason, the project team must be clear and honest about why the project has overrun its initial cost expectations and how that can be managed in such a way that the customer is clear about why the costs have exceeded initial projections.

If such cost overruns are due to additional customer requests, then it is easier to have the customer see the reasoning behind the additional cost. But if the cost overrun is due to some issue encountered by the project team, especially if it was an unforeseen issue, then the customer needs to be aware of it. However, cost overruns may not be absorbed by the customer, but rather, may be shared among the customer and team, or in the worst of cases, absorbed by the team especially if it is the team's responsibility.

Consequently, the ultimate goal of transparent communication is to ensure that all stakeholders in the project have a clear understanding of what is to be done, and where each party stands.

Cross functionality

One of the most important aspects of a Scrum team is cross functionality.

In short, cross functionality refers to being able to carry out different functions across the entire team. That implies that each team member would be able to do the same functions as the next member. While this may seem like overlap, it is quite useful particularly when you are considering the importance of having various team members support each other.

As such, cross functional teams are able to back each other up at all times especially when there is one team member that may be lacking expertise in a given area. Also, there are circumstances in which one team member has a specific skill set which is ideal for a given task.

In that regard, the entire team may rally around that individual and complete the required tasks. In addition, having strong team members in different areas will facilitate the work being done especially when other team members may be lacking that expertise.

Ultimately, a cross functional team is about utilizing everyone's talents and expertise in such a way that every team member is a valued contributor. Consequently, every team member is on the team because they have unique contributions to make which enhance the team's overall ability to perform and deliver on the project's objectives.

For instance, you may have a group of engineers. Since they are all engineers, they all share the same common training in the basics of engineering. But since they all have different specialties, they are able to support each other. So, you would have one engineer whose expertise is in structures, another whose expertise is in electrical, and so on.

The sum of this project team will allow them to design and construct a building without having overlapping functions and utilizing each of their individual skill sets. At the end of the day, this is the best combination of abilities and talents which you could hope for.

The right size of teams

One of the most common questions regarding Scrum is what the right size for a team should be.

The answer to this question depends on the scale and size of the project. To most outside observers, Scrum is seen as a limited proposition in which Scrum methodology can only accommodate one Scrum team per project. While we will be getting into scaling Scrum a bit later on, it is worth mentioning at this point that Scrum provides ample opportunity for scalability at much broader levels.

So, whether it is one Scrum team working on an individual project, or whether it is a group of Scrum teams working together on one larger project, each, individual Scrum squad does have a recommended size.

In essence, each Scrum squad should range somewhere between 4 to 8 members. Ideally, Scrum teams would have even numbers in order to accommodate for sectioning off a Scrum team into pairs if need be. This is an important consideration as Scrum advocates for collaborative work. Consequently, having odd-numbered teams would make it a bit more complex to section off work.

Also, having odd-numbered teams may end up promoting individual work since there is always one team member that would not have a pair. While it is not required for Scrum teams to work in pairs, it is a good idea for Scrum teams to encourage pair work. This is just another way in which Scrum teams can foster collaborative work.

Given the fact that 4 to 8 members is a good range, practice has shown that a good number is 6 members per team. This number of members would allow for the creation of 3, 2-member squads, while still having a manageable number of overall members. Another useful configuration of a 6-member team would be 2, 3-member squads.

The recommended minimum should be 4 members because 3 members may be too few members especially if a member leaves mid-way through a sprint. That would leave two members on the team, and of course, that may not be enough manpower to get through a sprint successfully.

If a team should have more than 8 members, the group a whole may be too large for a single Scrum Master to support. If a Scrum team needs to have more than 8 members, the Product Owner may consider having two Development Teams set, each with its own Scrum Master.

Of course, it is not as simple as just dividing up teams and getting additional Scrum Masters. There is a logistic constraint that would affect this proposition considering the fact that budgetary limitations may not allow for the hiring of additional team members or additional Scrum Masters. However, if the scope of a project is truly broad, then multiple Scrum teams may be the best way to go.

As such, 6 members seems to be the right size for a Scrum team as based on experience. It provides flexibility for the Scrum team, while providing a manageable team size that can work closely together and allow the Scrum Master a good, individualized attention scheme. Furthermore, 6-member teams can absorb the loss of a member much better than a 4-member team could. Teams greater than 8 members may also lead to a breakdown in the collaborative nature of the project as it fosters for subgroups to be formed within the larger project team.

Focus on commitment

An important trait that individuals need to share is commitment. For the team, as a whole, commitment means keeping a concerted, unified team effort in which the entire team can maintain a steady tempo.

Commitment also refers to ensuring that team members work in unison. Working in unison means knowing what everyone else is working on and also letting others know what you are working on. Ultimately, this boils down to transparency. Within a committed team, transparency opens the door to generate committed teams whose sole purpose is to further the accomplishment of the mission objectives set forth in the project.

In essence, the Scrum Master, as the coordinator of activities, needs to act as a type of "cheerleader" in such a way that individual team members are focused and committed on achieving the project's deliverables.

One important consideration on commitment is that the required traits for individual team members must be made aware of what is expected of them in terms of how they fit in the team as a whole. Consequently, individual team members who do not share the overall vision of the team may end up becoming a hindrance to the team's overall purpose.

Finally, it is imperative that the Scrum Master be a good role model in terms of their commitment to the team. In that regard, the Scrum Master leads by example so that the team, as a whole, can gain a deeper feeling of belonging and commitment. As the Scrum Master exhibits a committed attitude toward their team, the team will gain a greater sense of working together toward a common purpose in achieving the ultimate project aims.

Commitment is also a state of mind. Within the Agile mindset, commitment is all about delivering value to the customer and the end users of the final deliverables. As reflected in the Agile manifesto, delivering value to customers is the most important objective that Scrum pursues in every project. As such, this mindset is the ideal state under which a Scrum team should focus their efforts.

It is also worth noting that commitment is all about making sure that there is shared vision among all of the members of a project team. By having a shared vision, the project team can be sure that each task that needs to be completed is done in accordance to the overarching goals set at the beginning of each sprint.

So, it certainly pays to take the time to make sure that everyone is on the same page and working toward the same target.

Keeping a sustainable pace

One of the most important aspects of project management, in general, is maintaining sustainable pace in the development of a project. When you are unable to maintain a sustainable pace, you are setting yourself up for failure.

As such, it's important to note that it is vital for both a Scrum Master and Development Team to understand how long it realistically takes to get the job done. This is vital since an underestimation of time needed to complete a task could potentially become disastrous to the overall completion of the plan.

The best way to assess how long a task will take to complete is experience. Experience is the best way to determine how long a project will realistically take. However, there are cases when a project is completely new. In such cases, it may be hard to determine how long a project will actually take. Under these circumstances, it's important to overestimate the time that a project would take in order to complete a project. At the end of the day, it's worth buying your team more time. If you do have time leftover, you can always use this time to conduct testing.

Also, care needs to be taken in order to avoid sprinting out of the gate and running out of steam mid-way through the project. This type of mistake can easily be made when you are eager to get as much done is as brief a period of time as possible.

The main drawback with attempting to keep an unsustainable pace is that you run the risk of burning the team out. Of course, there may be times in which it is necessary to take things up a notch. But that can be a temporary situation especially when unforeseen issues come up. But this should only be a temporary approach.

In the long run, it's best for the Scrum Master to sit down with their team and work on a plan that will ensure a realistic tempo. For instance, it might be that one particular Scrum team is comfortable with working 10 or 12 hours a day. That might not be the norm, but it is not unheard of. Similarly, it could be that the Scrum team is rather inexperienced and might be more inclined to working an 8-hour day.

In the end, it's up to the Scrum Master to see how comfortable the team might be with working a certain number of hours and what the limits of that might be. Experienced Scrum Masters will have a intuitive feel for the way a Scrum team will be able to work based on the parameters of a given project. The main thing to keep in mind is that the overall tempo of a project should be dictated by the team and not by the Scrum Master. This will ensure the successful completion of the project within the schedule, and budget, that was intended.

Tolerance to failure

When we discussed the possibility of cancelling a sprint, the concept of failure was right in the middle of it. In essence, failure boiled down to being unable to complete the objectives set forth at the outset of the sprint. While the inability to complete objectives may not be the direct fault of the Scrum team, the end result does fall on the shoulders of the Scrum team.

As such, what can be done?

How can failure to achieve a task be dealt with?

The fact of the matter is that failure is nothing more than a learning experience. It is an opportunity to grow as a team and move on. Failure allows individual team members to learn from their experience and achieve a greater understanding of the way Scrum works and the way that the project-related tasks can be completed.

Now, failure is a positive so long as we're not talking about complete breakdown and failure to continue with the project. While cancelling a sprint may not be the end of the world, it should also be noted that we are not talking about shutting the entire project down.

On a deeper level, failure is a way of assessing the way a team is working. Under this assessment, the reasons for the failure can be determined and corrective measures may emerge from it. Perhaps the reason for the failure was a lack of expertise in one area, or perhaps it was due to inappropriate planning. Whatever the reason, the Scrum Master needs to sit down with their team and determine where things went wrong and what needs to be done in order to avoid it happening again.

Nevertheless, a line needs to be drawn at some point.

While learning failure leads to meaningful learning experiences, there is a point in which failure cannot be tolerated any further. It is at this point in which the Scrum Master, and a larger extent the Product Owner, need to make it clear that failure to deliver is unacceptable.

A good rule of thumb in this case is that failure should not be tolerated when it jeopardizes the completing of a sprint. Such failure may even doom the entire project's completion. As such, there should be no room for tolerance of such types of failure.

Again, there could be unforeseen issues which go beyond the control of the team. That much is clear. But if failure stems from negligence or just inadequate planning, then measure needs to be put into place in order to avoid further instances of such failure.

Ultimately, the best antidote to failure is conscious planning and commitment. By ensuring that planning is realistic and based on sound fundamentals, while having a committed team on board, then the chances of failure are greatly reduced.

Building a culture of feedback and continuous improvement

The final point in this chapter pertains to the importance of feedback.

Feedback is a crucial factor which can facilitate the achievement of project aims. Scrum teams should not be afraid of feedback. After all, negative feedback should be seen as a growth opportunity much the same way failure can be transformed into a positive outcome.

However, most individuals are afraid of feedback for fear of being judged in a negative light. But if things are going as well as they should, it is a great opportunity for all of the team members in involved to take a long look at one another and determine where things have gone wrong and where things can be improved.

Feedback, for better or for worse, can lead to continuous improvement.

If a team believes that everything it does is perfect, then they really are doing themselves a disservice. When you believe that everything you do is as good as it's going to get, then you are committed. You are not committed to improving and you are not committed to making the best of your opportunities to become better at what you do.

When you take feedback for what it is, it provides you with the opportunity to build on your current knowledge and experience. That can lead to improved performance in future projects down the road. Since you cannot expect to be perfect, you can always expect to improve upon your previous experiences.

How can you embrace a culture of feedback?

By being transparent and forthcoming.

There should be no need to be afraid of feedback if you are committed to doing things the best way you can and are committed to improving. That's it. That's all it takes.

Unless you are closed to improving upon your skills and your ability to continuously grow, then feedback can become an important ally for your team. Embrace the feedback received from customers; embrace the feedback received from peers, and certainly embrace the feedback which you can get from within your own team. The feedback that your own team can produce as a result of a self-assessment can go a long toward building a culture of excellence on all levels.

So, look at feedback as a valuable tool for your team's improvement and development. The Sprint Retrospective Meetings can be used to critique the work done in the previous sprint and how any shortcomings can be improved. And if there aren't any shortcomings to consider, then encourage your team to value new ways of doing things. You never know when you might come across a breakthrough. Such breakthroughs can lead to significant impacts on the same project, or future projects.

Chapter 4: Building a high-performance team

Scrum is all about high performance.

If your team does not perform at its best, then something is lacking. What this implies is that your team is not fully taking advantage of its skills and expertise.

Now, a high-performance team does not mean that you are furiously working long hours on end and producing massive amounts of results. A high-performance team is about producing the right results within the time and budget you determined at the outset of your project.

As we have highlighted throughout this book, building a great Scrum team is all about setting up the right culture among the team. If you are able to harness this culture, then you will be able to build a successful team around solid values and virtues.

At this point, it's worth underscoring the fact that the building of a strong team shouldn't be about finding a magic formula which can be used to produce results overnight. Rather, the right formula in this case is about building a culture from within which fosters development, creativity and an overall sense of purpose for your team.

When you are able to create this greater sense of belonging and commitment in your team, you are able to fulfill the expectations of your team at all levels. By fostering the feelings of commitment and belonging, you will be able to ensure that your team will be focused on getting the best possible results within the most reasonable terms.

Setting the right culture for creativity and collaboration

Setting up a good team culture is about setting up the Scrum team for success. When you are able to set up your team for success, you will be able to get the results you are looking for without having to sacrifice the individuality of each team member. This is important since every individual is capable of producing results and getting the most out of the opportunity they have to participate on the team.

Think of sports teams.

In team sports, positions are generally well-defined. That means that the players on the team have a clear idea of what they are meant to do and what they are expected to produce. When players don't have a clear idea of the position they are meant to play, then the results will speak for themselves. The players which have a keen understanding of the position they play and their role on the team are generally able to produce much better results. The reason for this is that they will not do anything that is not asked of them. Instead, they will do exactly what is expected of them. This implies that this clear understanding of their role gives them focus and purpose.

Also, you will hear about players being out of their natural position. What that means is that a player may be in a position which does not suit their individual talents and abilities. So, it's up to the coach to find the best way to get that player back into their natural role. By having a player outside of their natural role, the player is not being set up for success.

The same thing happens in any project environment. If the team member is not in a position in which they are comfortable and experienced, then they are setting themselves up for failure. Ultimately, this is not the type of failure which is conducive to learning. Rather, this is the type of learning which is conducive to destroying team morale and motivation.

This is where a Scrum Master must be a good judge of character and come up with the best way in which they can recognize when a team member is out of their element and in which cases a team member simply needs a nudge in the right direction.

With that in mind, Scrum Masters need to become familiar with the right ways in which they can motivate their team to constantly perform to the best of their capabilities. As such, we will be taking a look at an effective way in which a Scrum team can be effective and produce high-octane results on a consistent basis.

Using workshops to set the values for teams

At the outset of any project, a good Scrum Master will bring their team in for a meeting to plan out the work to be conducted throughout the entire project as divided up in each sprint and the subsequent work breakdown for each sprint.

This initial meeting is a great opportunity for setting up the ground rules of the project especially when team members are new to each other, that is, when team members are not familiar with one another. So, the Scrum Master has the opportunity to make things work in such a way that the entire team is on the same page from day one.

The ideal means of achieving this is through a workshop.

This workshop can be planned by both the Scrum Master and Product Owner, but ideally delivered by the Scrum Master. Now, it could be one workshop, or perhaps a series of workshops in which the team is familiar with what is expected of them and what they are expected to produce.

So, a good workshop should be oriented at providing a Scrum team with the foundation needed in order to perform at a high level.

Of course, all team members should be familiar with Scrum and Agile, and preferably certified to some extent in Scrum methodology. If a Scrum Master intends to use Scrum as the project methodology with a team that is unfamiliar with Scrum or has never worked with Scrum before, then a single workshop may not be enough to get everyone on board.

This workshop is intended to bring individuals, who are familiar with Scrum, together in a single environment so that they can work together toward a single end result.

The main objective of a pre-project workshop should be to establish the team's values. These values should be geared toward the successful completion of the project. It's that simple. If there are team members who are looking out for themselves and are reticent about working collaboratively, then finding a replacement for them before the project starts is the ideal time to do so.

When conducting a pre-project workshop, the Scrum Master should be looking to harmonize every individual's personal beliefs and attitudes so that the team can work toward the common goal of delivering value to the customer, early and often.

So, what would such a workshop look like?

Let's consider the following example.

Joe is a Scrum Master who has recently assembled a team of six members. The customer has hired the Scrum team to produce a marketing campaign for a new product launch. So, the Scrum team is made up of graphic designers, marketing experts, social media managers and a statistician.

Since the team members are new to the team, each member is unfamiliar with one another. So, there is a clear need to harmonize the team's efforts and direction in order to find a good rhythm for the team to perform. This is important since the fact that each member is unfamiliar with one another can lead to a steep learning curve.

So, the Scrum Master has assembled the team and taken some time to sit down with the team, as a whole, and go over what the project is about and what the final outcomes should be. But then, the next issue becomes: how to take a group of individuals and get them to become a cohesive unit that is dedicated to achieving a specific outcome?

That's where the magic of a good workshop comes into play.

At the outset of a project, the Scrum Master can bring his team in together for the initial project planning meeting.

During this meeting, the Scrum team meets for the first time. As such, it is very important to break the ice particularly if the team members are not familiar with one another. So, breaking the ice can be something as simple as having team members introduce themselves and talk about their experience. But this is only scratching the surface.

One of the mayor objectives of this project planning meeting should be to come away with a "playbook" of sorts. This playbook is intended to be the major guidelines for what the team is expected to do and how they plan to achieve it. Thus, the playbook can be a collection of techniques and strategies which can be used to achieve the project outcomes.

In our example, Joe has assembled a team of marketing experts who are familiar with the way a successful marketing campaign can be put together. So, the team has assembled to go over the major tasks that will be conducted throughout the life of the project. Also, they will discuss an estimation as to the overall amount of time the project will take.

Once the team has determined the major tasks that will be conducted and a general estimation of the overall time the entire project will take, the Scrum team can then move on to brainstorm ideas and ways in which each of the tasks can be completed. Also, the Scrum team can decide who will be responsible for each task.

This can lead to a very general work breakdown structure in which the main tasks to be covered in each sprint can be determined. This, in turn, leads to techniques and strategies being matched up with tasks to be conducted and the team member responsible for it. Consequently, the team is ready to get down to work and get things done.

So, what are the outcomes of this initial meeting?

1.   The team is aware of each member's strengths and experience

2.   The main tasks which need to be completed (there may or may not be user stories at this point, but just a general idea of what needs to be done in order to meet the customer's requirements)

3.   A rough estimate of how long it will take to get it done (unless the customer has fixed a specific amount of time)

4.   The number of sprints which may be required

5.   Who will be responsible for each task

6.   Techniques and strategies that can be utilized to achieve the main tasks

At this point, there are no specifics determined yet as this initial phase is intended to produce the main outline of what is expected to be produced at the end of the project. Most importantly, each team member already has an idea of how they will approach each task.

So, when the first Sprint Planning Meeting rolls around, each team member will know where they fit into the project and how they can approach the work that needs to be done in that initial sprint. This is especially important if team members are working with each other for the first time.

Consequently, having a clear idea of how the first sprint is going to be planned with allow the Scrum team to come up with a good way of approaching the work that needs to be done and what potential requirements may come about from needing to get this work done.

One final point about this initial project meeting: Scrum does not advocate for extensive documentation. So, how can you go about recording the topics discussed at this meeting without generating too much documentation?

The simplest way of recording all of this information is through a good, old-fashioned spreadsheet.

On a spreadsheet, the information discussed can be captured and distributed among team members is a format which is easy to read and easy to edit.

It may look something like this:

Task	Sprint	Strategies	Assigned to
Conduct customer survey	Sprint two	Skype calls, face-to-face meetings, phone interviews	Joe

As you can see from this example, tracking your team's progress doesn't have to be hard or complex. It can be solved by means of a simple spreadsheet focused on keeping score of what is agreed upon by all team members. And, of course, it is not set in stone meaning that it can be altered and modified as circumstances dictate. It could be that once you reach the Sprint Planning Meeting, the team realizes that someone else is more qualified than Joe to carry out this task. Or, it might be that the team has decided that this particular task is not needed in the project at all. Furthermore, the team may have decided that this task needs to be broken up into smaller tasks and so on.

Whateve r ends up being decided at the initial planning stages of the project serves as a guide for what will be covered in each,  individual sprint. But it's not until the team actually sit down to plan each, individual sprint, that the plans are finalized.

Nevertheless, the team is already clear on where it wants to go by the time it reaches the Sprint Planning Meeting. This provides clarity and a sense of direction for both the Scrum Master and the Development Team in order for them to gain a clear understanding of how the project's work breakdown structure will ultimately look like.

Determining what is important to your team

In the previous example pertaining to the workshop at the outset of the project, the team sat down and worked out what were the priority areas for the project. This means that the broad strokes of the work to be done were determined in addition to the main aspects to be addressed.

However, it is also up to the team to decide what is really important to them.

What does it mean to determine what is really important to them?

Well, think about it this way: the project team, while focused on delivering value to the customer, is focused on finding a new way of doing something which has already been tried and tested. This has become important to the Scrum team since they are eager to innovate and make a significant change in a rather traditional area.

While this may be an ambitious approach, the Scrum team feels that if they seek to innovate something which has been traditionally done in a certain way, they will be able to make a significant impact moving forward.

Such an approach can be underscored by something such as incorporating a new technology in something that has been traditionally done by hand. Or, it could be a new technology which supersedes a previous one. Perhaps the project team is eager to apply a new methodology that challenges the results of previous versions of the same methodology.

In this case, the Scrum team is committed to delivering value to the customer as usual, but the team has also determined that it is of value to them to try a new approach in the development of the new project deliverables. This implies that the team is also very eager to innovate.

In other cases, the Scrum team might be more concerned about getting the job done as fast as they can in order to have more time for testing. In this approach, the team has determined that testing is important to them since previous experience has shown them that a lack of testing led to a series of bugs once the product was released.

Ultimately, the project team needs to decide what they really want to get out of the project. And, they are free to do so as long as what they are aiming for is something that will contribute to the overall success of the project. It would make no sense for the project team to focus on aspects and areas which have no bearing on the overall completion of the project. For instance, the project team is more concerned about setting up a comfortable workspace rather than getting the job done itself. Such attitudes would lead to the project team becoming bogged down by unimportant details.

Using metrics to measure the product and the team

Metrics, and thereby measuring, are fundamental aspects of any project. When you set out on a project, your focus should be on quantifying the performance of the team and the effectiveness of the product being developed.

When the product is under development, testing can be done in order to determine if the product is living up to standards. In such cases,

229

problems and bugs can be caught during testing, fixed and then provide a quality product.

As such, it's rather straightforward on how to measure the effectiveness of a product.

What is not so straightforward is how to measure the effectiveness of the Scrum team.

In this aspect, it might get a bit tricky as to how to measure the overall effectiveness of the team. You might consider the following criteria to measure team effectiveness and performance:

- Number of user stories completed
- Tasks completed
- Incomplete/failed tasks
- Team turnover
- Number of bugs found
- Defects per parts
- Feedback

These are some examples of criteria which can be used to measure overall team performance.

For instance, the project contemplates a certain amount of user stories as reflected by the project itself. So, one sprint may include the completion of three user stories. However, the Development Team was only able to complete two.

In this case, the criteria indicate that the team had a subpar performance since they were unable to complete all three of the user stories planned for that sprint.

Of course, the question then becomes: why was the Development Team unable to complete all three user stories?

It could be that they ran out of time, there were unforeseen issues, team members left the project, and so on. Whatever the reason, the Scrum Master and even the Product Owner must determine what went wrong in order to correct it.

Also, the Development Team could be measured by the number of assigned tasks completed. If the Development Team is able to complete all of the tasks assigned to that individual sprint, then there is no doubt the sprint was successful. However, if there were incomplete tasks, then it boils down to determining which tasks were left incomplete and why.

Furthermore, the project team may be measured by the overall turnover in project staff. For instance, the team started off with 6 team members. By the end of the first sprint, two members had to be replaced. By the end of the second sprint, another two members had left, and so on. Perhaps it's just the one position that has constant turnover. Consequently, the Scrum Master needs to figure out why that specific position keeps generating turnover.

Now, if the project team should have zero turnover, then it might be considered a reflection on how well the team is run. In any event, the important thing to bear in mind is that the project team is able to complete the tasks that are assigned to them within the allotted period of time.

Notwithstanding, there is a certain level of quality which must be met by the Development Team in order to determine that the project has been successful. For instance, the project team may "complete" all of their assigned tasks, but the output is of such bad quality, that it is not functional as per specifications.

This also leads to the concept of defects per parts. This approach is typical to manufacturing in which quality is measure by the number of defects in a given amount of production. For example, you may have defects measured in parts per million, or perhaps in lines of code, or better yet, in each instance a service is provided.

And then there is feedback. This could be one of the most significant criteria used to measure a team's effectiveness. If the criteria show that a team was ineffective as perceived by the customer based on the final output, then that criteria can be used to determine the team was ineffective. If, on the contrary, the customer is thrilled with the final outcome of the product, then the team would be considered a success.

In much the same way a team's performance can be measured, so can the overall effectiveness of the final product. Its effectiveness can be measured in the way the product is able to solve the user stories or meet the customer's expectations.

So, you could have a product which meets all of the technical criteria, but that doesn't solve the actual needs of the customer. Or, you could have a fabulous product which checks off all the boxes and delivers the value the customer expects. This would mean that both the team and product have been successful.

Using a dashboard to track metrics

Determining which metrics to use in order to track progress is only the first step. The next step is to determine how to keep track of those metrics and also how to display them. That is where a dashboard comes in handy.

A dashboard can be as a simple as having a spreadsheet that tracks data and then displaying the final totals at the bottom of the page. This would enable the Scrum team to see the sum of the data and determine if it is producing what is expected.

Of course, dashboards can be far more complex. You might want to use gauges to visually represent the metrics that are being tracked much the same way a dashboard is outfitted in a car.

The main reason for using a dashboard is to have a visual representation of where the progress of the team, and the final product, are headed. This will enable all interested parties to see how things are coming along. As such, it ties into transparency and being forthcoming about everything that goes on in the project.

Best of all, by having a clear measure of the performance of a project, errors and efficient performance can be corrected ahead of time and in a clear and concise fashion. So, all team members can be on the same page and make the most of the important information which is displayed to the on the dashboard.

One very important note, updating the dashboard is just as important as updating the Scrum board. While the Scrum board specifically tracks the tasks that are completed and in progress, the dashboard tracks other data the project team considers important. Consequently, the lack of updates to the dashboard may result in having an incomplete picture of what is truly going on. So, it pays to make sure that the project data is being updated accordingly. This will enable all team members to be on the same page and allow the customer to be informed about where the project is headed.

Final thoughts

Building a high-performance team is no easy task. But the main point to keep in mind is that building a high-performance team is vital to ensuring the project's outcomes. Thus, when project deliverables are presented, all stakeholders in the project can be sure that such outcomes will meet their expectations.

By following the strategies outlined in this chapter, you can lay the groundwork for building a successful team that will be committed with the completion of the project and delivering the greatest amount of value that can possible be delivered.

This leads to a sustainable pace and committed attitude as the fruits of the Development Team's efforts become evident to the customer and to all stakeholders in the project. This is the reason why having up to date information is part of being transparent and honest. There is no need to hide information from anyone. But at the same time, it is also important that the data collection be congruent with the reality that the project team is actually living.

So, when your team sets out on a new project, your understanding of what your team expects and what they value will help you build a successful team that will win every time. All you have to do is know exactly what to look for in each player and make sure they are in the right spot on the team.

Chapter 5: Getting everyone on board... and keeping them there

Thus far, we have talked about getting the right people on board and getting them on the same shared vision. We have had an in-depth discussion on all of these aspects throughout this book. But, believe it or not, we still have lots more to discuss.

You see, building the right team isn't just about magically finding the right staff. It's about really knowing what you are looking for and going down that road. After all, not all personalities are the same and not all folks would be able to gel on the same team. That's a fundamental point since having talented individuals, but who don't really get along, may be a detrimental for the team as having folks who have no clue about what they are doing.

So, there must be a happy medium right?

In fact, there is. That is why we are having this discussion in this chapter. Throughout this book, we have discussed how important it is to get a shared vision which is conducive to building the right team culture and enabling the entire team to become successful on a large scale. However, we haven't touched upon how to actually assemble the right team members.

Often, it is not easy for Scrum Masters and Product Owners to find the right team members. After all, the core of any successful Scrum-based project is to find the right people which can comprise the team and thereby make a successful Scrum team.

But, where can you find these folks?

Most importantly, how can you determine if they are the right folks for the job?

These are questions which you can answer by taking a deeper look at your project's vision and philosophy.

On the surface, we have discussed the main traits that team members ought to exhibit, such as, being open minded, committed and detail oriented. Nevertheless, how can you determine if a given individual stacks up accordingly?

You can usually tell if a potential team member is right for your team if they are willing to buy into your project's vision. When you develop this vision, you can then "sell" it to potential team members. The more they buy into the vision and underlying philosophy, the easier it will be for you to attract the right team members.

You can build your project's vision and philosophy by using a structured approach such as the "Product Canvas."

The Product Canvas is just that, a canvas, which displays the main aspects of the project in a visual format which can enable any observer to get a clear picture of where the project is going, what it is about, and what needs to get done.

Many times, Product Owners and Scrum Masters have trouble getting their vision for the project across because they are unable to truly articulate their thoughts. By utilizing a graphic organizer, it is a lot easier for potential team members to make a clear assessment if they can deliver, or not, on this project.

The Product Canvas has the following sections:

1. The goal
2. The metrics
3. The target group
4. The big picture
5. The product details

These are the components of the Product Canvas. When you are able to put all of these aspects together, you are able to create a holistic vision for your final product which can be easily articulated and transmitted to the project team, or any outside observer. This is especially important if you are seeking outside sources of funding for your project, or if there are addition project stakeholders that you need to bring on board.

That being said, the Product Canvas acts as a dashboard that can be permanently displayed and consistently used as a reference for the duration of the project.

Now, let's discuss each of these items in greater detail.

- **The goal**. This is the main objective of the project. In short, it is what you are trying to achieve with the final outcome of your project. This could realistically be anything that you are striving to achieve. For instance, it could be to boost sales, increase the number of subscribers, or just introducing a brand into the market. Whatever the objective, it must be a clear depiction of the reason for creating the final product.

- **The metrics**. These metrics do not pertain to the development of the final product, but rather to the performance of the final product. For instance, if your goal were to create an app which will increase the number of subscribers to your company's service, then the clearest metric would be the number of new subscribers your app has generated. Let's say that you are looking to increase the amount of sales, then your metric would be the actual dollar figures attached to those sales via the use of the app.

- **The target group**. This one is fairly straightforward. This section refers to the end users of the final product you are creating. These users are represented by the user stories you have created for the final version of the product.

- **The big picture.** This aspect refers to the process that it will take to reach the final outcome you have set for your project. This refers to the actual design process, the development of the final deliverables and how the final product will be tracked in order to determine if the project's overall scope has been successful. With this, you can keep a constant track of where the lifecycle of the project is heading.

- **The product details**. These items will serve as a tie-in for the following stages of the product's development. As such, this will enable you to see where the next steps lie in the product. For instance, you could be looking at tracking specific product features to see how they impact the overall performance of the of final deliverables. You may end up finding out that the features which you thought would generate the most impact did not while other seemingly less important features were the ones that generated the greatest amount of impact.

As you can see, the Product Canvas is a rather complete approach which you can use to make the most out of your product planning and get your project's objectives of the group. The main thing to bear in mind is that the end user, that is the customer that will actually benefit from the outcomes of this project, should be at the forefront of the efforts intended in the project's development. Furthermore, the project team needs to be aware that the customer who is behind the project itself, in addition to other project stakeholders, needs to be put at the forefront of the development stages. Hence, the Development Team truly finds itself in at the service of those for whom the project is intended.

Creating a Scrum team

The development of the Product Canvas is a great start to the project. In fact, it is highly recommended to have this canvas set up prior to the hiring of Development Team members. The reason for this is that when a potential member is considered for the team, they will know exactly what is expected of them and what they need to do in

order to meet the objectives of the project.

As such, the Product Canvas can either be developed by the Product

Owner, or by the Product Owner and the Scrum Master in tandem. I have also pointed out that the Scrum Master may choose to develop this canvas with the Development Team especially in those cases where the project's outcomes have not been developed before. Thus, the Development Team may have the required skills and tools that the Scrum Master and the Product Owner may lack.

In such cases, it would be recommended that the Product Canvas be developed with an experienced team that has either worked together before or has had some exposure to Scrum and Agile. When the Development Team are experienced, it is easier to avoid setbacks since the team knows where it is going and has a better understanding for what the Agile and Scrum worlds will require of them.

Assuming that the Scrum Master, or Product Owner, has already developed the canvas, then they can go out to find the right members for the team. Getting these team members on board boils down to finding the folks with the right attitude, the right skill set and of course, who agree with the compensation package attached to their participation in the project.

Compensation of team members is always a sticky subject.

After all, how can you determine how much a team member should earn?

That depends on a number of variables, such as, your budget. Also, it might boil down to your ability, or lack thereof, of procuring enough funds to even pay the Development Team a competitive wage. This is where having people buy into your project's philosophy becomes one of the most important aspects of the project's vision.

Therefore, Development Team members have to be committed with the project's vision especially if their initial compensation may not be as attractive as expected. Your project's compensation structure may be tied to the overall product's success. So, if the final product is successful, the team gets paid. If it fails, then the team essentially works for nothing,

An "all or nothing" approach may be a bit too much for some folks to stomach. So, they may not buy into the project's vision. But you may find folks who are willing to give their time and efforts in building a project which won't pay off in the short run but has the potential to pay off considerably in the long run. These folks may be driven to build something worthwhile which would ultimately lead the to gaining far more than if they had gotten paid for the work up front.

Determining the right members

Consequently, the right team members are those who are committed to the project's vision. It should be said that if you are hiring employees to go along with the work that needs to be done in order to produce your project's final outcomes, then you will get employees.

What does that mean?

It means that employees will do what they do in exchange for a salary. They won't be committed to producing the right outcome. They will only be concerned with doing the bare minimum in order to get the job done and collect their pay. That's it. They won't be committed with doing their best. While they may be committed to learn and gain experience, employees won't give their all for the sake of the project.

So, the right team members are those who are personally committed with the outcomes. It could be that it boils down to a personal commitment with the other individual team members. It might be that this project offers an individual to work on something they have always wanted to work on. Or, it might even allow a team member the opportunity to prove to themselves, and thereby everyone else, that they are capable of working at a given level.

So, these various motivations are important for you to understand when assembling your team. If you are looking for employees, then you will get folks who are in it for the money. Plain and simple. But if you are looking for folks who are truly motivated and will have a personal interest in making their contributions really count, then your project must give them the opportunity to shine, especially if they haven't had the opportunity to do so before.

Ultimately, your team should be able to offer everyone the opportunity to contribute equally in such a way that all team members are partners. This is the reason for the flat structure. If you allow individual members to feel like employees, then you are opening the door for team members to feel undervalued and underappreciated. At the end of the day, this will kill your team's motivation and drive.

How to select the right members

Once you have figured out the opportunities that your project has to offer, you can use that as a "sales pitch." This pitch isn't about offering people opportunities for growth and learning in lieu of payment. Sure, if you can afford to pay people so that they can pay their bills, then do so. They will appreciate the income. But if beyond the income there are opportunities to grow and develop skills which are useful to them, then you have a valuable proposition for individual team members.

By the same token, you also need to have a clear checklist of what you are looking for. That checklist may include the hard and soft skills that are required for the successful completion of your project. After all, you might have committed individuals but who lack the technical knowledge needed in order to carry out the project itself. Therefore, you would have to make a choice, would this team member's lack of experience of technical know-how be offset by their attitude.

Consider this situation.

You are looking for engineers to work on a construction project. As such, you are looking for individuals who are committed to building the structure, but who would have to be willing to accept a lower than market compensation structure.

Consequently, this compensation structure may attract younger, less experienced engineers who are looking to get their feet wet in the business. As such, are you willing to accept less-experienced engineers who are looking to gain experience?

If you find that you cannot afford to have less experienced staff, then you might have to up your compensation structure in order to attract more experience and knowledgeable engineers. But if you feel comfortable with that type of on-the-job-training situation, then you could perfectly consider hiring less experienced engineers, but who have a solid technical background as learned in college.

Now, I will say this: often having less experienced people on a project may lead to greater innovation. The rationale behind this statement is that it is often seen that more experienced folks tend to have a way of doing things. Therefore, if a team member is set in their ways, then Agile may seem a bit extreme for them. Thus, your project team may not fully embrace change and innovation as well as you hope they would.

At the end of the day, the selection of the right team members boils down to the personalities which would mesh the best with the overall philosophy and scope of the project. If you find that folks are approaching your team because they are hoping to get paid, then you might have to find other folks who might be less concerned about money (even though they would need the paycheck), but who are more concerned about gaining experience and making the most of their opportunity to participate in a project such as yours.

Selecting the right Scrum Master

The choice of a Scrum Master is just as critical as that of the individual team members.

If your choice for Scrum Master is a "boss," then you might be in trouble. The Scrum Master is not anyone's boss. In fact, under the Scrum umbrella, there are no bosses. There are just team members working together toward a common goal. That's all.

If your perception of a Scrum Master is all-knowing, fearless leader, then you might have the wrong vision in mind.

A Scrum Master is, by definition, a subservient leader. This means that as a project leader, the Scrum Master puts their team ahead of themselves. This is a crucial aspect to a Scrum Master. If your choice for a Scrum Master is not willing to put the team ahead of themselves, you might be setting your team up for an unpleasant situation.

Now, having such a person is not necessarily a bad thing; it's just that that is not the Agile mindset. Having such a personality "running" things might be better suited for a more traditional project management approach, in which case, you might consider a different project management approach.

Also, the Scrum Master should be someone who is knowledgeable and understands the way Scrum and Agile work, but who is also knowledgeable in the way the actual product works.

Consider this: you know of a very experienced Scrum Master. This person has ample experience in software development but hasn't worked on marketing projects before. So, you can't be sure that this Scrum Master's experience will translate into a successful marketing campaign. There is a chance that it would, but odds are it may not.

So, this is why selecting the right Scrum Master, with the right profile, may prove to be the hardest task of all. Your choice of a Scrum Master will ultimately boil down to finding a committed individual, who is happy with the compensation structure, and is able to check their ego at the door.

This is just like sports.

The best team players are the most talented individuals who are also willing to play as a team and make the most of their participation on the team.

When they enter the game, they know that they have the chance to be difference-makers, but at the same time, they are willing to give others around them the opportunity shine. You can see this when these stars pass the ball to the other players as opposed to expecting others to pass to them first.

This attitude is what can certainly make, or break, the overall performance of your team. So, please be aware that your choice of Scrum Master is just as important as any other team member you need to choose. Your choice for Scrum Master needs to be as committed, or even more so, than the rest of the members of the project team.

At the end of the day, everyone is on the same boat. No more, no less. So, it's worth making the most of their time on the boat.

Chapter 6: Running a sprint

At this point, you should have all of your project planning done and your Scrum team all set and ready to go. So, the biggest issue now becomes getting your project off the ground.

Scrum, as compared to other project management methodologies, breaks a project's development into sections called "sprints." For experienced Scrum practitioners, sprints represent intermediate steps that build on each other. Consequently, the process by which the project team is able to build the final outcome allows for a gradual and incremental approach in building the project.

This is an important aspect to take into account since building the project progressively allows the project team to consider which aspects are susceptible to improvement as each sprint wears on.

In that sense, each one of the sprints produces an outcome which then serves as the basis for the next sprint. However, each sprint also allows the Scrum team to consider the mistakes and problems encountered as a part of the previous sprint.

This is one of the key differences in Scrum as opposed other non-agile project management methodologies. When you run a project through a series of successive sprints, you are able to correct the mistakes, bugs and any other issues before the final testing of the product.

This is a direct byproduct of the Agile manifesto.

In the Agile manifesto, working software and value to the customer are an essential part of the process throughout the entire lifecycle of the project.

So, that implies that the project team must be able to deliver value to the customer at the end of each sprint. While "working software" refers specifically to an IT or software-related project, the concept of delivering value at the end of each sprint represents a cross-cutting approach which can be applied to any project.

Consider this example:

A construction company is building a road. For the sake of simplicity, the company has broken down a 10-mile road into 10, one-mile sprints. As such, the outcome of each sprint is intended to deliver a one-mile stretch of road which is perfectly usable at the end of the sprint.

So, this implies that at the end of all 10 sprints, the entire road will be completed.

Thus, the end of each, individual sprint delivers "working software," in this case, a road.

Under traditional project management methodologies, the value to the customer would not be delivered until the end of the project, that is, at the end of all 10 miles. While this is a traditional approach utilized with projects such as road construction, the fact of the matter is that is there was a design flaw, or some other type of mistake during the construction process, it wouldn't be addressed until the end of the project. This is why it is so common to have construction projects delivered only to find flaws and design issues.

Once the project is completed, correcting issues may be virtually impossible. As such, construction projects may end becoming useless since it is too late to address any potential issues. This is why it is common to find that public works end up becoming costly mistakes.

So, when it comes time to getting your project off the ground, it certainly pays to take the time to really plan out the activities which will be conducted in each sprint and how this can be utilized to get deliver value to the customer as early as possible in the project's lifecycle. While this means that you may not be able to deliver working software at the end of the very first sprint, you might be able to deliver value very early on as opposed to waiting all the way to the end of the project to do so.

Envisioning

In this first step of the planning process, the project's vision may be created. This is where the Product Owner sits down and puts the project's vision together. So, this may imply that you, as a Product Owner, or as a project sponsor, will think about where the project should be headed.

At this point, the Product Canvas really becomes a useful tool.

In an earlier chapter, we described how the Product Canvas can be utilized to develop a vision which can be "sold" to potential team members. This project vision is vital in getting the people on board for the project. If you are not able to articulate your vision in a tangible and visual manner, your project may well be doomed from the start.

When you are developing your vision, the Product Canvas becomes the springboard for the final product's development. The Product Canvas will be able to help you determine what needs to be done, when it needs to be done and for whom it needs to be done. So, let's drill down on some of the finer points of the Product Canvas which were not discussed in the previous chapter.

Product name

The final output of your product needs to have a name. Whatever it is, it will most likely be called something. So, determining that name early one is useful, but not an absolute necessity.

Think of films and books.

Often, films and books have a working title. This is the title by which writers have produced the original draft or script by which the film is shot, or the book is edited.

Somewhere along the way, a director or studio executive may choose to change the title. Perhaps there's a line or scene in the movie which provides the inspiration for the final name of the film. Perhaps there is an event in the movie's production that forces the name change. Perhaps it boils down to marketing and how marketing the movie is much easier under a different title. Whatever the case, the working title may end up being dropped in favor for a different title.

The same thing happens with book publishers. Often, publishers may not be enamored with the title of a book and choose to change it during the editing process. While writers may not agree with the title, it is the ultimate decision on the part of the publisher since they are the ones who will be printing the book.

In that regard, your product's name may be changed as a result of the development process. Perhaps your Development Team may come up with a better, cleverer name for the product. It might end up being better than you could have imagined. Or, it could be that you just couldn't think of a name, and as a result of the development process, your team has come up with a good one.

In the end, whatever you choose to call the work in progress should give your team a clear idea of what they are working on. Something vague such as "Project X" won't cut it. Unless you are working on a top-secret military project, your best bet is to find a working title that makes sense to your team. So, if you are developing a fitness app, a good working title might be, "Fit 2 go." If that sounds corny, your team can always come up with something different.

The project vision

So, the use of the Product Canvas is all about generating the vision for the project. However, it is often useful, and necessary, to articulate your product's vision into one statement which encompasses the entire value being developed throughout the project lifecycle.

Consequently, you may have a project statement such as, "bridging two communities." This statement would apply to actually building a physical bridge between two communities, or perhaps bridging communication between two communities. In either case, you are making an emphasis on the fact that you are bridging communication. No more, no less.

The canvas itself allows all stakeholders to have a clear idea of where the project is going at all times.

How the canvas is actually presented depends on the nature of the product and of the stakeholder. Personally, I like to have two versions. One, a digital version which can be shared through Google Docs or some other type of file sharing format. The other could be a print version which can be displayed on a board or pinned up on a wall.

In either case, the canvas should be visible to everyone so that they are able to have a constant reminder of where they are going and what the end result of the project is going to be. Also, having the canvas up on display will allow everyone to be constantly reminded of what they are working toward. It is incredible how having a constant reminder of what you should be doing and why you are doing it allows you to keep your focus while reducing the likelihood of distraction. It also helps the project team to cut out any tasks that are not related to the individual sprint or the project itself.

Product backlog and sprint backlog

Once the project vision has been developed and properly shared, it is time to develop the Product Backlog.

The Product Backlog is essentially a collection of all of the tasks which will be completed throughout the lifecycle of the project leading up to the ultimate completion of the final product. The Product Backlog depends on the number of sprints that will be run and the amount of time each sprint will last.

These parameters are not standard and really depend on the aspects of each project. For instance, you might have four weeks to complete a project. And, given the scope of the project, you might feel that one, four-week sprint would be enough to get the job done.

In other cases, the customer may leave it up to you decide how long the project will take. So, you could approach it in one of two ways.

Firstly, you base your decision on your experience. You have done similar projects in the past. So, you are aware of how long it will take to get the job done given a certain set of conditions. This might be your most accurate way of measuring how long the final product will take especially if you don't have specific time constraints.

The second approach could be to have your project team assembled and make the decision based on a realistic assessment of all of the project members. In this case, you would take everyone's opinions into account in order to determine what needs to be done and when it should be done.

Under this approach, you would determine the number of sprints, the length of each sprint and then proceed to create the Product Backlog based on the feedback given by your team. Ultimately, you would be able to determine the tempo at which the project would be run and what kind of pace your team would need in order to get the job done within the time frame they have decided.

So, if you have a team that works faster as compared to other comparable teams, you may be confident in reducing the time needed in order to get the project done. In other cases, you might have a more inexperienced group which would motivate you to take on more time to complete the final outcome.

A good rule of thumb is that sprints generally last from two to four weeks. Given that all projects are different, the project team would have to figure out what the best length for a sprint would be. As such, a two-week sprint might work best, or perhaps a six-week sprint. It all depends on what the actual project is about. But on the whole, a good rule of thumb seems to be four weeks.

My advice would be to consult sprint lengths with your team whenever possible. Unless you have time and / or budgetary constraints that limit the amount of time you have to complete a project, the best way to go about it would be to ask your team how fast they could get the job done and base your timing decisions on that.

Learn fast and pivot

Often, there will be mistakes made in the early stages of a project. This is especially true when you are not familiar with a particular type of project. So, it is always a good idea to fail early and get those mistakes out of the way. In doing so, you will be able to find your bearing early on. The worst thing that can happen is not addressing issues early on only to have them grow into something much larger in the latter stages of the project. So, it is always best to be willing to fail early on and learn the lessons which will allow your team to get the most out of their experience.

One very important point is that tolerance to failure should be seen as the result of a learning experience. This tolerance is based on the normal course of business in a project. However, truly, large-scale mistakes should be avoided at all costs.

Consider this situation:

Your team is designing a new car. The requests from the customer call for a lighter vehicle which you have a smaller engine and thereby improving fuel economy. So, your design team comes up with a lighter frame which enables it to put in a smaller engine. However, initial estimates were off, and the car actually weighs more than intended. And since you chose a smaller engine, it now turns out that the car doesn't have the same power and acceleration as originally intended. But since this project was conducted under a traditional project management methodology, the team didn't realize this mistake until the first prototypes were built.

When the results of the initial testing were brought forth to the company executives, they were given two choices. One, go back to the drawing board and alter the frame, or put in a bigger engine. The company executives decided to axe the project as they felt safety features would be compromised by a lighter frame and putting a bigger engine in would not meet the fuel economy standards that the company wants to offer its customers. So, by axing the project, the work done by this team goes up in smoke.

In this example, the team made a catastrophic mistake which led to the demise of the project at the testing phase. Had someone caught on to that mistake early on, then the project might well have been saved. But since they didn't, the project was a complete failure.

With this example, the intent is to provide a greater understanding of how a project should be managed given the circumstances which it might be under. As such, failure, so long as it does not jeopardize the project itself, should be taken in stride.

Great sprint planning

Now that you have the overall scheme of where your project is headed, it's time to plan your first sprint. In order to plan a sprint, the Scrum team takes part in what is known as the Sprint Planning Meeting.

During this meeting, the Scrum team creates the Sprint Backlog. The Sprint Backlog feed off the original Product Backlog, that is, it chooses which tasks from the overall Product Backlog will be completed in that sprint.

Naturally, the first sprint would have all tasks available to it. This would mean that the Scrum team needs to be very careful in deciding which tasks will get done first. If you are planning subsequent sprints, then you would have a reduced number of tasks available given that some might have already been completed.

With that in mind, the Sprint Planning Meeting provides the team with the tasks that will go into the work breakdown structure that actually tells individual team members what they will do in each sprint.

The Scrum Master can then track progress on the Scrum board and the Scrum Burndown Chart. The Burndown Chart is simply a visual tool which tells the team how much time there is left before the sprint is completed. This allows the Scrum team to focus and not waste any time.

As such, the Sprint Backlog provides the team with the objectives it needs to complete at the end of the sprint. It is simply up to the Scrum Master to make sure that progress stays on track throughout the duration of the sprint.

Release planning

Since the aim of each sprint is to produce working software, there needs to be a set of criteria which would determine what needs to be done in order to achieve a product release. This could be a set of criteria which determine the functionality of the product.

Consider this example.

The team is developing a new medication. At the end of a sprint, the new medication will be ready for animal testing. However, it needs to meet the technical criteria determined to be needed in order to have it approved by the official government regulatory agency for animal testing. If these criteria are not met, then the drug will not be approved for animal testing and the deadline will not be met. On the other hand, if the deadline is met, then the drug will proceed on to the next stage and everyone comes up a winner.

This end result can only be achieved by careful track of the project's progress and grooming of the backlog. This implies that the backlog will reflect what has already been done and what needs to be completed. At the end of the day, the remaining tasks will reflect the need of the project based on the overall conditions the project is under.

The example of a new medication underscores one very important aspect: certain projects will have to meet with requirements that go beyond any requirements the customer can make. Rather, those requirements may come from government agencies or regulatory bodies. In which case, the project team needs to have that in mind in order to determine the project's overall success rate.

Furthermore, each sprint should get closer and closer to the ultimate release of the final, finished version of the product. Thus, when the final product is eventually released, it will be fully compliant with all requirements thereby greatly reducing the chance that the project will not pass the standards it will be held up against.

Optimizing a sprint

As with anything in Scrum, it is subject to optimization. That means that there is always room for continuous improvement. Even if you think that something cannot be improved, there is always some room from improved functionality.

As such, running a sprint is no different.

First off, the Daily Standup Meeting provides an opportunity for feedback on a daily basis. This implies that the Scrum team would have a chance to go over their daily work and see where things may be improved, or perhaps cut out, based on the fact that there are mistakes or negative conditions to be rectified.

The Daily Standup Meeting also allows for team members to voice any concerns about the direction the project is headed and what can be done to deal with such situations. Perhaps there is a team member that is not pulling their weight. Or, one piece of vital equipment is not working properly. Perhaps there are unforeseen circumstances which are holding the team back. Whatever the case, this meeting allows for feedback on a daily basis.

So, it's important for the team to create a feedback loop. The Scrum Master may provide feedback on the way they see how things are going while the team can provide feedback based on their perception of the way things are going. The main thing to keep in mind is that there is no need to be afraid of feedback, rather, it is certainly worthwhile to be honest and forthcoming about the way things are going. At the end of the day, feedback allows for assessment and greater understanding of how the overall process is going.

The Sprint Review Meeting

Once the end of a sprint has been reached, the team will hold what is known as the Sprint Review Meeting. In this meeting, the team will present their latest advancements to the customer. The customer will then be able to see the product's functionality at that stage of the project.

For example, the project is at a point where the project is ready to be tested, but it does not have the full set of features that the final version of the product will have.

Consider the example of a car.

The car has been fully built and can be road tested. The car is fully functional in the sense that it has a frame, powertrain and certain safety features, but does not include the full set of features such as the final paint job, accessories and other electronics. The reason for conducting a road test at the end of the sprint is to show the customer what the vehicle can do in terms of its performance. In later sprints, the full range of features will be added so that the customer can see what the finished product will look like.

At this point, the customer can give their blessing so the team can move on to the next stage, or perhaps critique the release of the product so that the team can go back and make changes as per the customer's request.

The main purpose of this meeting is to get feedback. Of course, if everything is perfect, then there would be no need to worry about changes to the product. But if feedback suggests there should be changes made, then the team still have time to right the ship before the final release of the product.

The Sprint Retrospect Meeting

During the Sprint Retrospect Meeting, the Scrum team has the chance to sit down and go over what was done, and what wasn't, during the previous sprint. This is a space for open and honest commentary so that each member is aware of what they are doing, and how they could improve upon their work.

In addition, it also allows for the customer's feedback during the Sprint Review Meeting to be incorporated in the upcoming Sprint Planning Meeting. While there may be a number of issues to discuss, the Sprint Retrospect Meeting, as all meetings in Scrum, should be short and to the point. Once the main issues have been cleared up, then the Sprint Planning Meeting should incorporate the reflections and feedback from the previous sprint.

Personally, I like to have the Sprint Retrospect Meeting segue into the Sprint Planning Meeting as all of the items discussed are fresh and at the forefront of everyone's minds. If you choose to let some time in between both meetings, you might end up missing the point of the feedback your received. Thus, it is always a good idea to address issues while they are fresh in everyone's minds.

Once you have gone through feedback and any issues Scrum team members encountered in previous sprints, you would then be ready to kick off your next sprint. And then, the entire process repeats itself. This is why Scrum is considered to be iterative as the same process repeats itself over several times throughout the course of the project's lifecycle.

Ultimately, your efforts to foster continuous improvement stem from your ability to take the feedback which has been provided to you by your customer and team and incorporate it to your planning down the road. In doing this, you are ensuring that your team feels that their voices are being heard while you can rest assured that you are trying to your best to address any and all potential issues before they become a potential problem.

Chapter 7: Scaling up Scrum

One of the biggest criticisms is that Scrum is not scalable. That means, that it is not suited for large projects. However, that criticism is unfounded, and it is rooted in a lack of knowledge and understanding on how Agile works.

Agile essentially works like any other project management methodology. If there is a large-scale project which needs to be completed, it can be blown up to meet such proportions. If the project is small and does not require a vast amount of resources, then Agile and Scrum can suit those small projects, too.

The reason for this belief is that Agile was born out of the software industry. So, many non-Scrum practitioners believe that Scrum cannot be scaled and thereby lacks the necessary elements of truly large projects.

Well, what would count as a large project?

How about constructing a building?

A building, as a structure, has several elements and components. For example, digging up the land, laying the foundation, building the structure, doing the interior, electrical, plumbing and roofing, and any other specific components such as elevators or escalators.

Every one of the components previously mentioned could well be run by an individual Scrum team. For instance, the foundation requires a considerable amount of manpower and resources to complete. So, your construction site supervisor can work as a Scrum Master. The supervisor would be to use each of their individual construction workers as members of the Development Team. Each member has their own role to play and will provide their own contributions to the project.

Now, the Scrum Master, or supervisor, reports to the project engineer (the Product Owner) who is in constant touch with the customer and project sponsors. This communication allows all of the stakeholders in the process to know if the project is on track or falling behind.

Once the foundation has been laid down, the same group of workers could transition into the structure team. Perhaps these workers are specialists in laying down foundations and would not be a part of the structure team. In which case, the structure team would be a separate Scrum team. In any event, there is a supervisor acting as a Scrum Master with the project engineer acting as the Product Owner.

Also, it could be that each sprint corresponds to one floor being built. So, the project team estimates that it can finish a floor in a week. So, if the building has 15 floors, then the structure itself would take 15 weeks.

Then, another Scrum team, the electrical and plumbing would come in and set everything up. They also estimate that they would be done with one floor per week. However, the are not going to wait until the structure team is done. They will get started once the first floor is done. That way, the interior team will be one week behind the structure team.

Now, the customer can be called in at the end of each sprint, that is, once the foundation has been laid. And then, after the structure on the first floor is done and then after the interior has been done and so on. In reality, the customer only needs to see one floor once as the remaining floors would all be the same.

This example clearly underscores how Scrum is not only adaptable to any industry, but it can be scaled as needed.

In fact, when the construction project reaches a point where multiple Scrum teams are working at once, the project engineer will have multiple supervisors working at the same time. This makes the project engineer the Project Product Owner. The Project Product Owner may choose to name a Project Scrum Master, which would be one

Scrum Master coordinating the work of the individual Scrum Masters.

And just like any other Scrum project, there are Sprint Review Meetings and Sprint Retrospect Meetings. In this example, the supervisor can call his workers in for a short meeting and just go over any issues they may be having. For instance, the weather isn't cooperating, and workers are being negatively affected by it.

Such simple aspects can go a long way toward providing useful feedback thus ensuring the overall quality of the project.

Scrum of Scrums

When dealing with larger Scrum teams, a technique called a "Scrum of Scrums" can be used in order to manage the daily tasks of such a large group. Unlike the previous example, a Scrum of Scrums does not have multiple teams with multiple Scrum Masters. This concept considers having one large team which is divided into subgroups. This plays off the initial consideration we had about maintaining ever-numbered groups.

Let's consider the following case.

A Scrum team consists of 16 members given the size and the scope of the project to be completed. The budgetary restrictions do not allow for individual Scrum teams, say, two teams of eight, or even three teams of six. So, there is one Scrum

Master and one Product Owner looking after all 16 members.

In order to make the division of labor much easier, the Scrum Master has divided the 16 members into four subgroups of four. Each subgroup is intended to cover a specific amount of work during each sprint.

Since the Scrum team has a Daily Standup Meeting, the Scrum Master has to make a choice: does the Daily Standup Meeting include all 16 members of the team or could the meeting include less members?

There is one problem with each approach.

In this first approach, having all 16 members may drag out the meeting far longer than necessary. Each member may have something to say and that, in itself, may lead to some disorganization in the meeting. So, the meeting could ultimately become counterproductive.

The second approach, working with less individuals poses a problem since it would be difficult to choose who is in the meeting and who isn't. One workaround could be to designate a "group lead" and have this person attend the daily meetings. That would reduce the amount of participants from 16 to 4. But that poses another issue: Scrum does not advocate "leaders" or folks "in charge" within each group. Bear in mind that Scrum has a flat structure meaning that everyone has equal participation.

So, what's the solution?

A Scrum of Scrums.

In a Scrum of Scrums, each of the members of the subgroup gets a chance to represent the team at the daily meeting. Since everyone is equally involved in the process, everyone would be equally qualified to represent the group at the meeting. A good rule of thumb is to rotate reps every day. Unless sprints were unusually long, rotating reps every day makes the most sense.

Now, it could be that a sprint would take 8 weeks. In such a case, the team might decide to rotate reps on a weekly basis. That might work insofar as giving each member the opportunity to handle the responsibility of attending the meeting on a more permanent basis.

Now, the one consideration under this approach is to avoid having one "permanent" rep. The whole point of avoiding a permanent person representing the group boils down to avoiding having any semblance of hierarchy within the Scrum team. As such, having a rotating representation is the best way to go.

Ultimately, the point of having such a set up is to reduce the likelihood of one team member taking over the rest of the group. While there are folks who are more naturally inclined to a leadership role, the fact of the matter is that by having rotating roles, you are able to make sure that everyone gets equal participation thereby fostering a collaborative approach within the team.

Scaled Agile framework

So, when Agile is scaled up to a larger framework, keeping track of the workflow and making sure that the collaborative nature sticks gets harder and harder. So, it then becomes a challenge for Scrum practitioners to enforce a discipline whereby team members have equal participation, work is conducted in as per the user stories outlined at the beginning of the sprint, and the overall nature of the project is completed within the aspects pertaining to the Agile mindset.

As such, large projects can be perfectly accommodated within an Agile framework with the basic difference that the ultimate work breakdown structure as seen in the Product Backlog and the individual Sprint Backlogs may be divided among individual teams rather than one collective work divided among individual team members.

In order to make this concept resonate on a deeper level, consider the following situation:

A food manufacturer wants to produce a new low-calorie drink. Since the market is demanding low-calorie drink options, the management team at this corporation is looking to produce a low-calorie drink which can compete with other brands in similar categories.

Consequently, a team has been assembled in order to determine the right formula for this new drink. The company has decided to invest in research and development into producing a new drink rather than just rebadging an existing one.

So, the CEO of the company has called in one of the company's production engineers and named them "project engineer." This engineer is aware of the value in the adoption of a Scrum approach to this project. As such, the project engineer has assumed the role of Scrum Master. The client is the CEO who has been designated by the company's board as the person in charge of making sure the project comes to fruition.

Thus, the project engineer comes in a decides to build multiple Scrum teams that can work at once especially since the company has determined that a proposal for a new drink needs to be ready before the holiday season. In this case, the project would have about three months to be completed. This means that there is no time to be wasted.

The Scrum Master, or project engineer, decides that the best course of action is to assemble a research team which can look into the actual production of the drink, a production team which can look into the logistics of bottling and distribution and a marketing team which can come up with a brand name, graphics and art for the sole purpose of producing the new drink.

All three teams will work in tandem in such a way that they are all in a concerted effort toward producing a new, low-calorie drink.

The Scrum Master has decided to coordinate each team through a Scrum of Scrums approach. Under this approach, the main idea is to ensure that the all of the teams are working in tandem thus moving the project along with multiple groups working in sync.

In every sprint, each of the groups works on the same user story, except from their own angle. So, the user story is based on a consumer who is young and is looking for a low-calorie option which can help them cut down on their sugar consumption while maintaining the flavor of other drinks on the market.

At the end of each sprint, all three teams present their advances. The research team presents their results in the development of the drink, the production team indicates how they will approach the product while the marketing team unveils their plans for the drink.

Ultimately, the entire team arrives at the same destination with a finished drink, distribution and production considerations in check, and a solid marketing campaign in place. The final presentation of the product is presented to the company's board. The project is approved by the board and is ready for an official product release, that is, a formal launch into the marketplace.

This example underscores the fact that in order to tackle a rather large project, the project engineer, or Scrum Master, decided to find the best way to come up with a new drink and set it up in the market. Whether or not the product is a success once in the market remains to be seen. The most important thing to keep in mind is the need for the project team to find the best way to work on the project in a collaborative manner which underscores the needs and requests of the customer thus delivering value at all times.

Coordinating multiple Scrum teams

In the previous example, we were able to see how multiple Scrum teams can be coordinated through the use of a Scrum of Scrums. While using multiple Scrum Masters might be a good solution, it might not be the most practical when taking budgetary restrictions. The previous example highlighted how the company wanted a new low-calorie drink and just tapped one of their best engineers to take on the project.

While the project engineer could have found a traditional approach and used a regular methodology to exert influence, the fact is that the new drink might not have been ready in time for the launch. The reason for this is the interdependency among tasks. Under a traditional approach, the project team would have to wait for one team to be done before the next team could begin.

Sure, this approach would provide a more "predictable" outcome, the fact of the matter is that traditional project management methodologies are used to produce predictable results. When something such as the creation of a new product requires the intervention of a project team, then there is a clear need for the each of the members to find the best way to make their work count. That is why Scrum can be used across a number of different industries and fields.

The fact that Scrum has a cross-cutting appeal, it allows project managers to find an effective way of running a number of teams simultaneously. This implies that the project team is able to make sense of the various tasks that need to be done in such a way that the project team is able to get a firm grasp on the various objectives that need to be completed throughout the lifecycle of the project.

Moreover, being able to use Scrum in a scalable fashion allows for greater flexibility as opposed to a rigid, traditional project management approach that forces project managers to delay certain portions of a project until one portion is complete.

For instance, a traditional project management methodology would not allow all three teams to run simultaneously. The project team would have to wait until there was a successful formula developed for the drink while the remaining teams might be able to come up with ideas but wouldn't be able to work until the previous step had been developed.

Distributed Scrum teams

One of the most important factors in a Scrum project is finding the right way to manage multiple teams working at the same time. Ideally, these teams would be distributed evenly at the same physical location. This is the concept of co-location, and according to Scrum doctrine, it is the best way in order to ensure that teams are working collaboratively.

But what happens if there are teams distributed in different geographical locations?

Is it possible to run a sprint when team members are not physically located in the same place?

The answer is yes.

Modern technology has facilitated communication in such a way that teams can work in different geographical locations and still achieve positive results. The fact that Scrum teams can communicate via the internet allows for teams to work remotely without having to bridge the distance by moving and thereby increasing the cost of the project.

However, such an approach is not for everyone.

Some folks can work perfectly fine on their own. They are capable of producing results without having someone looking over their shoulder to see what they are doing. Then, there are others who are not so adept at working on their own. They may find themselves in a situation in which they need to have someone telling them what to do in order to get things done.

While Scrum does not advocate telling people what to do, the psychological pressure of having a team working around them helps them to focus on getting work done. Nevertheless, using Scrum to work with teams located in different geographical locations is possible.

Yet, there is one limitation. Such projects need to be those which can be assembled over the internet, or which do not require the production of a physical good. In such cases, there would be a point where team members would have to come together to produce the actual, physical good.

Consequently, part of the project could be done remotely, and part of the project would have to be done in person. Under these circumstances, project teams would be able to make sense of their tasks without necessarily having to be together at all times.

How and when this approach is used depends largely on the nature of the project. So, it's up to the project manager to find the right way to make sure that the project team can work despite distance and other considerations that may negatively affect the team's overall performance.

The use of Scrum in maintenance projects

At this point of the book, we have discussed how Scrum is used to create value especially when there are new products being produced. Yet, we have not discussed what happens in the case of such projects where there is nothing new being created, but maintenance is the primary focus.

One such example could be an update to an existing product. This update could be commissioned by the customer or stakeholder in order to fix bugs found in a project.

Consider this situation:

An automobile manufacturer has realized that one of their recent models has been shown to have transmission problems. So, the automobile manufacturer has decided to commission a Scrum team to find a good solution to the transmission issues for this vehicle.

In this example, the project team is not actually developing anything new. They are just finding corrective measures to a problem which has been identified after the release of the final product. Now, you might think, "why wasn't the problem detected?"

The reason for something such as this could be due to the fact that testing did not reflect the true conditions under which the final product was going to be used. So, even though the initial project team tested the new car's transmission, they were unable to determine how well it would hold up under normal circumstances.

The end result was the need to fix the transmission for upcoming models to be released.

The Scrum team has come together, run several sprints, detected the problem and proposed a corrective solution. The latter sprints were intended to provide more thorough testing to the new transmission so as to avoid the same problems the previous transmission had. In the end, the results were positive, and the new transmission has been cleared for new models.

This example underscores how it is possible to use Scrum even when you are not exactly producing anything new. It could be that fixing a faulty transmission required a minor tweak in the overall design of the device. Nevertheless, a Scrum team was able to find it and make sense of how it can be improved.

Bear in mind that Scrum is all about continuous improvement. So, these types of projects are specifically aimed at producing such continuous development, not just in the production of new projects, but in improving upon existing ones.

Conclusion

So, we have arrived at the end of this journey through the world of Scrum and Agile. I hope that you have found this book to be useful and informative.

If you have made it this far it is because you are truly interested in making the most of your experience as a Scrum practitioner. If you are new to the Agile world, then I am sure you have walked away with a greater and deeper understanding of how Agile can become a feasible way in which you can produce high-impact projects in a logical and congruent manner.

As such, I would encourage you to get your feet wet in the world of Agile. I assure you that once you see how effective Agile can be, you will not go back. Scrum is the most powerful Agile methodology you can find today. It is not only the ultimate concentration of viable projects, but also the best way in which you can find the means to produce results that will make your projects successful every time you take the field.

As always, please don't forget to comment on this book. There are other interested folks who are looking to learn more about Agile and Scrum, and how these methodologies can help them improve their own knowledge and acumen in the project management world.

Also, please share this information with your colleagues and business associates, or anyone who would be interested in the world of Agile. I am sure that they will find this book to be useful in helping them build their own understanding of the Agile world and how they can improve their own projects. I am sure that they will appreciate learning from you as well.

See you next time.